The Craft of Multicolor Knitting

BARBARA G. WALKER

Photography by William J. Williams

CHARLES SCRIBNER'S SONS · NEW YORK

Contents

Printed in the United States of America
Library of Congress Catalog Card Number 73-3008
SBN 684-13405-5 (paper)

Glossary of Terms and Abbreviations

I. BASICS

K—Knit.

P—Purl.

St—Stitch. Sts—Stitches.

B—Work through the back loop of the stitch. "K1-b" means: knit one stitch through its back loop, inserting the needle into the stitch from the right-hand side. "P1-b" means: purl one stitch through its back loop, placing the right-hand needle point behind the stitch as if to insert the needle between the first and second stitches from the back, then inserting it, instead, into the *back* loop of the first stitch from the left-hand side, and wrapping the yarn around the needle point in front to complete the purl stitch as usual.

Sl—Slip. To pass a stitch or stitches from the left-hand needle to the right-hand needle without working them. The right-hand needle is always inserted into a stitch that is to be slipped *as if to purl* (i.e., from the right-hand side), unless directions specify "as if to knit" or "knitwise" (i.e., from the left-hand side).

Sl-st—Slip-stitch. A stitch that has been slipped.

Wyib—With yarn in back. Used with slip-stitches, it means that the yarn is carried across *behind* the stitch, on the side of the fabric that is *away from* the knitter. Whether this is a right or wrong side makes no difference.

Wyif—With yarn in front. When a stitch is slipped, the yarn is carried across in *front* of the stitch, on the side that is *facing* the knitter.

Rep—Repeat.

Rep from *—Repeat all material that comes after the *, in the same order.

( ) Parentheses—Indicates a repeat of material within the parentheses (or brackets) as many times as specified immediately after them; i.e., "(k2 tog, k1) 3 times" means: k2 tog, k1, k2 tog, k1, k2 tog, k1.

II. DECREASES

K2 tog—Knit two stitches together as one stitch.

P2 tog—Purl two stitches together as one stitch.

K2 tog-b—Insert the needle from the right into the back loops of two stitches at once, and knit them together as one stitch.

P2 tog-b—Turn the work over slightly and insert the needle from the left into the back loops of the second and first stitches, in that order, then wrap yarn around needle in front to complete the purl stitch. Same action as "p1-b" performed on two stitches at once. NOTE: In some circumstances, and for some knitters, "p2 tog-b" is awkward to work. The same effect can be obtained if desired by working the two stitches in the following manner: p1, sl the resulting st back to left-hand needle, then with point of right-hand needle lift the *next* stitch over the purled st and off the left-hand needle; then sl the same st back to right-hand needle and proceed. This is like a "psso" in reverse.

Sl 1, k1, psso—Slip 1 st wyib, knit 1 st, and pass the slipped stitch over; that is, insert the point of left-hand needle into the slipped stitch and draw it over the knit stitch and off the right-hand needle.

Ssk—Slip, slip, knit. This abbreviation is used almost always throughout this book, *instead of* the more usual "sl 1, k1, psso", because it is shorter, less easily confused with "sl 1, k2 tog, psso", and when done as directed makes a neater-looking decrease. Work "ssk" as follows: slip the first and second stitches *knitwise,* one at a time, then insert the tip of the left-hand needle into the *fronts* of these two stitches from the left, and knit them together from this position. (If, after trying this, the knitter still prefers to use "sl 1, k1, psso" for every "ssk", it is quite permissible to do so.)

Double decreases—These are k3 tog, p3 tog, k3 tog-b, sl 1—k2 tog—psso, all of which are self-explanatory; and p3 tog-b, which can be worked as described above under "p2 tog-b", by purling two stitches together, returning the resulting stitch to the left-hand needle, and passing the next stitch over. A double decrease makes 1 stitch out of 3.

Sl 2—k1—p2sso—This is a double decrease that is used when it is desirable to have the central stitch prominent. It is worked as follows: insert the needle into the fronts of the second and first stitches on the left-hand needle, as if to k2 tog; do not knit these stitches together, but *slip* them, both at once, from this position. Knit the next stitch on left-hand needle, then insert left-hand needle point into *both* slipped stitches at once and draw them *together* over the knit stitch and off right-hand needle, just as in "psso".

III. INCREASES

Inc—Make two stitches out of one, by knitting into the front and back of the same stitch. This also may be done purlwise, by purling into the front and back of the same stitch, or it may be worked by (k1, p1) into one stitch, or (p1, k1) into one stitch.

M1—Make One. A method of adding a new stitch without leaving a hole or bump. Unless otherwise specified, it is done as follows: insert needle from behind under the *running thread* (which is the strand running from the base of the stitch just worked to the base of the next stitch) and lift this thread onto the left-hand needle; then knit one stitch into the *back* of it. "M1" can also be done purlwise, by purling into the back of the running thread, or by other methods which are explained in the patterns where they occur.

Knit next st in the row below—This is an increase *only* when followed by "then knit the st on needle". To knit in the row below, instead of working the loop that is *on* the needle, work into the loop that is immediately *under* the needle—i.e., the same loop that was on the needle in the preceding row. "Purl next st in the row below" is done the same way.

Yo—Yarn over. Take the yarn over the top of the needle once before making the next stitch. If the next stitch is to be knitted, then the yarn is simply taken over the top of the needle to the back, where it is in position to knit. If the next stitch is to be purled, then the yarn is taken over the needle to the back, then under the needle to the front, where it is in position to purl. (Note: English knitting directions distinguish between these by calling a yo before a knit switch "wf"—wool forward—and a yo before a purl stitch "wrn"—wool round needle.) A yo also may be worked in reverse: i.e., under the needle to the back, then over the needle to the front. This reverse yo is sometimes used on purl rows.

(Yo) twice, yo2, or 00—All these mean the same thing: a double yarn-over. The yarn passes over the needle to the back, under the needle to the front, and over the needle to the back again before making the next stitch, so that there are *two* extra strands on the needle. A double yarn-over is usually worked as two new stitches on the return row, by working (k1, p1) or (p1, k1) into the long loop.

(K1, yo, k1) in next st, (k1, p1, k1) in next st, (k1, yo, k1, yo, k1) in next st—these are various ways of making three or more stitches out of a single stitch. All material within the parentheses is to be worked in the *same* stitch before passing on to the next one.

IV. GENERAL

RT—Right Twist. Skip 1 st, knit the second st, then knit the skipped st and sl both sts from left needle together.

LT—Left Twist. Skip 1 st, knit the second st in *back* loop, then knit the skipped st in front loop and sl both sts from left needle together.

MB—Make Bobble. Usually done by increasing in one stitch, then working short rows on the increased stitches. Methods vary according to pattern.

Turn—This means that the work is turned around in the knitter's hands *before* the end of a row, to work some distance backward over the most recent stitches.

Short row—This is the knitting that is done after a turn, before continuing the original row.

Drop stitch—A stitch dropped off the needles, to be picked up later.

Dip stitch—A new stitch created by knitting into the fabric some rows below the stitches on the needle. Usually it is worked together with the next stitch on left needle.

Half-drop—A method of arranging pattern motifs all over the fabric, by working the first half of the pattern rows in one repeat along with the second half of the pattern rows in the adjoining repeat.

Slip-Stitch Color Patterns

Many knitters like to use the "Fair Isle" method of forming designs in color, changing the colors as required for each stitch, and stranding the unused colors across the back of the fabric. But there are no patterns for "Fair Isle" knitting in this book. "Fair Isle" knitting is plain stockinette stitch, with no texture interest; the designs are made only by alternating colors.

Slip-stitch color knitting, on the other hand, presents true stitch patterns which are embellished and enhanced by contrasting colors. It is easier for the novice to master, because it does not require careful regulation of tension. It does not even require two yarns of the same weight and thickness. Exciting effects can be obtained by combining not only different colors, but also different textures of yarn: a heavy-weight with a lightweight, a wool with a cotton, or a standard yarn with a ribbon. Metallic yarns, too, can be combined with the non-glittering kind to make delightfully dressy fabrics. These patterns are to *create* with. Modern knitting yarns offer a wide variety of colors, textures, and fiber types to work with; and slip-stitch color patterns offer an equally wide variety of wonderful ways to put them together.

Even if you have never tried patterns of this type before, you will have no difficulty in understanding them and using them. There is nothing to remember about the knitting technique except the distinction between "wyif' and "wyib". *Front* is always the side of the knitting that *faces* you as you knit, and *back* is always the side that faces away from you. It does not matter whether you are looking at the right or wrong side. Colors are changed at the end of a row, simply by dropping the strand that was just used and picking up a different strand from below. Thus, no strands ever have to be cut or broken. It is a good idea to drop the old strand in *front* (i.e., toward the knitter) of the new one, so that all will be woven neatly around the side edge of the finished knitting.

No black-and-white picture can do justice to a pattern that is intended to be worked in color. So it is particularly important in color work to take up yarn and needles, and actually try the patterns. You will like the rapidity and ease with which most of them can be worked, and you will enjoy seeing the design as it should look—that is, colorful!

Ridge Check Pattern

Slipped-stitch ridges, translated into two colors, make this beautiful easy-to-work check that goes well in any sweater, jacket, skirt, or dress. The long slipped stitches carry each color upward against a stripe of contrasting color.

Multiple of 4 sts plus 3. Colors A and B.

Row 1 (Wrong side)—With A, purl.
Rows 2 and 4—With B, k3, * sl 1 wyib, k3; rep from *.
Row 3—With B, p3, * sl 1 wyif, p3; rep from *.
Row 5—With B, purl.
Rows 6, 7, and 8—With A, repeat Rows 2, 3, and 4.

Repeat Rows 1–8.

Ridge Check Pattern

Blended Stripes

The unusual touch here is the working of slip-stitches on the purl side of the fabric, which imparts enough tension to prevent curling, and makes a nice firm knit piece. Since the purled colors alternate on every row, the stripes are blended together at the edges. This is a "beginner's pattern", useful for almost any kind of garment.

Multiple of 4 sts plus 3. Colors A and B.

Cast on with Color A and knit one row.

Row 1 (Right side)—With B, k1, * sl 1 wyib, p3; rep from *, end sl 1, k1.
Row 2—With B, k1, * sl 1 wyif, k3; rep from *, end sl 1, k1.
Row 3—With A, p3, * sl 1 wyib, p3; rep from *.
Row 4—With A, k3, * sl 1 wyif, k3; rep from *.

Repeat Rows 1–4.

Blended Stripes

Long-Slip Stripes

Contributed by Hildegard M. Elsner, Aldan, Pennsylvania

This pattern looks nicest when worked in many colors, using the same 4 rows for each color in turn. Because of the long slip-stitches, the fabric will curl while the work is in progress; but it can be pressed flat when finished.

Odd number of sts. Colors A and B.

Cast on with Color A and purl one row.

Rows 1 and 3 (Right side)—With B, k1, * sl 1 wyib, k1; rep from *.

Row 2—With B, p1, * sl 1 wyif, p1; rep from *.

Row 4—With B, purl.

Rows 5, 6, 7, and 8—With A, repeat Rows 1, 2, 3, and 4.

Repeat Rows 1–8.

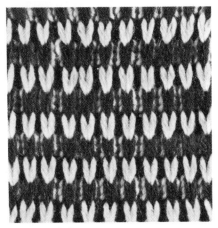

Long-Slip Stripes

Bean-Sprout Pattern

This is a simple and pretty little "dot" design with some of the dots elongated and others not. To reinforce the suggested springlike theme of young shoots, work it in green and yellow, or in two shades of green.

Multiple of 6 sts plus 5. Colors A and B.

Row 1 (Right side)—With A, knit.

Row 2—With A, purl.

Row 3—With B, k2, * sl 1 wyib, k1; rep from *, end k1.

Row 4—With B, k1, * (k1, sl 1 wyif) twice, p1, sl 1 wyif; rep from *, end k1, sl 1, k2.

Rows 5 and 7—With A, k5, * sl 1 wyib, k5; rep from *.

Rows 6 and 8—With A, p5, * sl 1 wyif, p5; rep from *.

Rows 9 and 10—With A, repeat Rows 1 and 2.

Row 11—With B, k1, * sl 1 wyib, k1; rep from *.

Row 12—With B, k1, * sl 1 wyif, p1, (sl 1 wyif, k1) twice; rep from *, end sl 1, p1, sl 1, k1.

Rows 13 and 15—With A, k2, * sl 1 wyib, k5; rep from *, end sl 1, k2.

Rows 14 and 16—With A, p2, * sl 1 wyif, p5; rep from *, end sl 1, p2.

Repeat Rows 1–16.

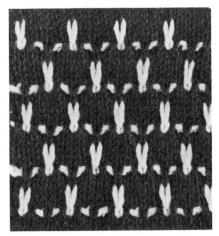

Bean-Sprout Pattern

Black Forest Pattern   *See color page i*

This three-color variation on the endlessly-variable Three-and-One theme comes from southern Germany and Austria. It makes charming sport sweaters, caps and mittens for children or adults, and is so easy to work that it might well serve as the beginner's first attempt at a three-color garment.

Multiple of 4 sts plus 3. Colors A, B, and C.

Row 1 (Right side)—With A, knit.
Row 2—With A, purl.
Row 3—With B, k3, * sl 1 wyib, k3; rep from *.
Row 4—With B, p3, * sl 1 wyif, p3; rep from *.
Row 5—With C, k1, * sl 1 wyib, k3; rep from *, end sl 1, k1.
Row 6—With C, k1, * sl 1 wyif, k3; rep from *, end sl 1, k1.
Rows 7 and 8—With B, repeat Rows 3 and 4.
Row 9—With A, repeat Row 5.
Row 10—With A, p1, * sl 1 wyif, p3; rep from *, end sl 1, p1.

Repeat Rows 1–10.

Carrousel Check   *See color page i*

Here is a very attractive three-color pattern that is easy to work, novel, and striking. It makes a firm, non-curling fabric that is suitable for almost any type of garment. It is gay enough for children's wear, yet sophisticated enough for high-fashion clothing.

Multiple of 8 sts plus 5. Colors A, B, and C.

Cast on with Color C and purl one row.

Row 1 (Right side)—With A, k5, * sl 1 wyib, sl 1 wyif, sl 1 wyib, k5; rep from *.
Row 2—With A, k1, p3, k1, * sl 1 wyif, sl 1 wyib, sl 1 wyif, k1, p3, k1; rep from *.
Row 3—With B, k1, * sl 1 wyib, sl 1 wyif, sl 1 wyib, k5; rep from *, end last repeat k1 instead of k5.
Row 4—With B, k1, * sl 1 wyif, sl 1 wyib, sl 1 wyif, k1, p3, k1; rep from *, end sl 1 wyif, sl 1 wyib, sl 1 wyif, k1.
Rows 5 and 6—With C, repeat Rows 1 and 2.
Rows 7 and 8—With A, repeat Rows 3 and 4.
Rows 9 and 10—With B, repeat Rows 1 and 2.
Rows 11 and 12—With C, repeat Rows 3 and 4.

Repeat Rows 1–12.

American Beauty Tweed   *See color page ii*

This pattern is the opposite of English Rose Tweed, although it alternates colors in the same way. Instead of a loose fabric, the American Beauty makes a tight, dense one, suitable for coats and other outdoor garments. It is cheerful and gay when worked in three bright, strongly contrasting colors; subtle when worked in three different shades of the same color.

Multiple of 4 sts. Colors A, B, and C.

Cast on with Color A and purl one row.

Row 1 (Right side)—With B, k1, * sl 2 wyib, k2; rep from *, end sl 2, k1.
Row 2—With B, k1, * sl 1 wyib, sl 1 wyif, p2; rep from *, end sl 1 wyib, sl 1 wyif, k1.
Row 3—With C, k3, * sl 2 wyib, k2; rep from *, end k1.
Row 4—With C, k1, * p2, sl 1 wyib, sl 1 wyif; rep from *, end p2, k1.
Rows 5 and 6—With A, repeat Rows 1 and 2.
Rows 7 and 8—With B, repeat Rows 3 and 4.
Rows 9 and 10—With C, repeat Rows 1 and 2.
Rows 11 and 12—With A, repeat Rows 3 and 4.

Repeat Rows 1–12.

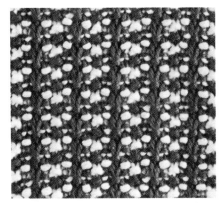

Color-Seeded Pattern

Color-Seeded Pattern

Basically Seed Stitch, this pattern shows the novel use of purled stitches on the right side, to make a scattering of color spots. The exceedingly simple technique gives a flat, firm, non-curling fabric.

Multiple of 4 sts plus 3. Colors A and B.

Row 1 (Right side)—With A, p1, * k1, p1; rep from *.
Row 2—With A, repeat Row 1.
Row 3—With B, p1, k1, p1, * sl 1 wyib, p1, k1, p1; rep from *.
Row 4—With B, p1, k1, p1, * sl 1 wyif, p1, k1, p1; rep from *.

Repeat Rows 1–4.

Dovetail Stripes

Multiple of 4 sts. Colors A and B.

Cast on with Color A.

Rows 1 and 3 (Right side)—With B, k2, * sl 1 wyib, k3; rep from *, end sl 1, k1.

Rows 2 and 4—With B, k1, * sl 1 wyif, p1, k2; rep from *, end sl 1, p1, k1.

Rows 5 and 7—With A, k1, * sl 1 wyib, k3; rep from *, end sl 1, k2.

Rows 6 and 8—With A, k1, * p1, sl 1 wyif, k2; rep from *, end p1, sl 1, k1.

Repeat Rows 1–8.

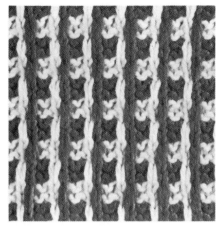

Dovetail Stripes

Two-Tone Lattice

Contributed by Hildegard M. Elsner, Aldan, Pennsylvania

Here an ordinary check pattern is transformed into a superbly graceful latticework design by the simple expedient of straining stitches—that is, by stretching the same pairs of slip-stitches over 4 rows instead of the usual 2. As is always the case when stitches are so treated, the fabric is very dense and sturdy. Use this pattern to make a beautiful pair of mittens, or a sofa cushion in your choice of decorator colors. A third color can be introduced, if desired, on Rows 5 and 6.

Multiple of 6 sts plus 2. Colors A and B.

Cast on with Color A and knit one row.

Row 1 (Right side)—With B, k1, sl 1 wyib, * k4, sl 2 wyib; rep from *, end k4, sl 1, k1.

Row 2—With B, p1, sl 1 wyif, * p4, sl 2 wyif; rep from *, end p4, sl 1, p1.

Row 3—With A, repeat Row 1.

Row 4—With A, k1, sl 1 wyif, * k4, sl 2 wyib; rep from *, end k4, sl 1, k1.

Row 5—With B, k3, * sl 2 wyib, k4; rep from *, end sl 2, k3.

Row 6—With B, p3, * sl 2 wyif, p4; rep from *, end sl 2, p3.

Row 7—With A, repeat Row 5.

Row 8—With A, k3, * sl 2 wyif, k4; rep from *, end sl 2, k3.

Repeat Rows 1–8.

Two-Tone Lattice

Twice-Turned Check

Twice-Turned Check

This easy-to-work pattern makes a firm, flat, close fabric for suits, coats, cushions, casual dresses and sweaters. The slipped stitches are the ones that are "twice-turned"—the first time by the way in which they are twisted when slipped, the second time by being knitted through the back loops. As a result the pattern takes on an appearance of small cross-hatched diagonals, though in fact there are no such diagonals because the slip-stitches really go straight up.

Odd number of sts. Colors A and B.

Row 1 (Wrong side)—With A, knit.
Row 2—With B, k1, * keeping yarn in back, insert needle from the *left* into the *back* loop of next st, as if to p1-b; *slip* the st from this position; k1; rep from *.
Row 3—With B, k1, * sl 1 wyif, k1; rep from *.
Row 4—With A, k1, * k1-b, k1; rep from *.
Row 5—With A, knit.
Row 6—With B, k2, rep from * of Row 2; end k1.
Row 7—With B, k2, * sl 1 wyif, k1; rep from *, end k1.
Row 8—With A, k2, * k1-b, k1; rep from *, end k1.

Repeat Rows 1–8.

Ribbon Bow

Ribbon Bow

This is a charming, easy-to-work pattern for little girls' dresses, baby sweaters, and dainty blouses. The Color B yarn resembles a ribbon woven vertically through the fabric and tied at intervals. Rows 1 and 2 can be worked with real ribbon, instead of yarn, for an especially pretty effect.

Multiple of 4 sts plus 3. Colors A and B.

Cast on with Color A and purl one row.

Row 1 (Right side)—With B, k1, * sl 1 wyib, k3; rep from *, end sl 1, k1.
Row 2—With B, k1, * sl 1 wyif, k1, k1 wrapping yarn 3 times, k1; rep from *, end sl 1, k1.
Row 3—With A, k3, * sl 1 wyib dropping extra wraps, k3; rep from *.
Row 4—With A, p3, * sl 1 wyib, p3; rep from *.
Row 5—With A, k3, * sl 1 wyib, k3; rep from *.
Rows 6, 7, and 8—With A, repeat Rows 4 and 5, then Row 4 again.

Repeat Rows 1–8.

Pearl Tweed

Here is a very novel tweed pattern with a gentle diagonal line and a horizontal accent formed by the strands woven across the front of the fabric. It is an excellent pattern for coats, suits, sweaters, and skirts.

Multiple of 3 sts plus 2. Colors A and B.

Cast on with A and purl one row.

Row 1 (Right side)—With B, k1, * sl 2 wyif, k1; rep from *, end k1.
Row 2—With B, p1, * k1, p1, sl 1 wyif; rep from *, end p1.
Row 3—With A, k3, * sl 1 wyib, k2; rep from *, end sl 1, k1.
Row 4—With A, purl.
Row 5—With B, k2, * sl 2 wyif, k1; rep from *.
Row 6—With B, p2, * sl 1 wyif, k1, p1; rep from *.
Row 7—With A, k1, * sl 1 wyib, k2; rep from *, end k1.
Row 8—With A, purl.
Row 9—With B, k1, sl 1 wyif, * k1, sl 2 wyif; rep from *, end k1, sl 1 wyif, k1.
Row 10—With B, p1, * sl 1 wyif, k1, p1; rep from *, end p1.
Row 11—With A, k2, * sl 1 wyib, k2; rep from *.
Row 12—With A, purl.

Repeat Rows 1–12.

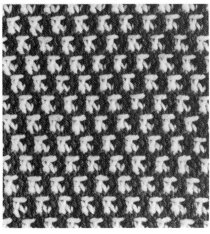

Pearl Tweed

French Weave, Plain and Fancy

Here are two patterns that incorporate the same two-color motif; a small diamond-shaped figure with a short woven strand of contrasting color in the center. In the Plain version, a lattice-like design, this motif is clearly seen. In the Fancy version the pattern goes off-center, to make an intricate and interesting series of diagonal lines; but the little diamonds are still there. Both versions are easy to work.

I. FRENCH WEAVE, PLAIN

Multiple of 4 sts plus 3. Colors A and B.

Row 1 (Wrong side)—With A, purl.
Row 2—With B, k1, sl 1 wyif, k1, * sl 1 wyib, k1, sl 1 wyif, k1; rep from *.
Row 3—With B, p3, * sl 1 wyif, p3; rep from *.

ABOVE: *French Weave, Plain*
BELOW: *French Weave, Fancy*

Row 4—With A, k1, * sl 1 wyib, k3; rep from *, end sl 1, k1.
Row 5—With A, purl.
Row 6—With B, k1, sl 1 wyib, k1, * sl 1 wyif, k1, sl 1 wyib, k1; rep from *.
Row 7—With B, p1, * sl 1 wyif, p3; rep from *, end sl 1, p1.
Row 8—With A, k3, * sl 1 wyib, k3; rep from *.

Repeat Rows 1–8.

II. FRENCH WEAVE, FANCY

Multiple of 5 sts plus 4. Colors A and B.

Row 1 (Wrong side)—With A, purl.
Row 2—With B, k1, sl 1 wyib, * k1, sl 1 wyif, k1, sl 2 wyib; rep from *, end k2.
Row 3—With B, k1, p1, * sl 1 wyif, sl 1 wyib, p3; rep from *, end sl 1 wyif, k1.
Row 4—With A, k3, * sl 1 wyib, k4; rep from *, end k1.
Row 5—With A, purl.
Row 6—With B, k2, * sl 2 wyib, k1, sl 1 wyif, k1; rep from *, end sl 1 wyib, k1.
Row 7—With B, k1, sl 1 wyib, * p3, sl 1 wyif, sl 1 wyib; rep from *, end p1, k1.
Row 8—With A, k5, * sl 1 wyib, k4; rep from *, end last repeat k3.

Repeat Rows 1–8.

Woven Block Stitch

This is a very easy-to-work pattern that is particularly attractive in coats or jackets. It can be worked in three colors: the first 14 rows with A and B, the second 14 rows with A and C—and so on, alternating colors in the woven bands.

Multiple of 9 sts plus 4. Colors A and B.

Row 1 (Right side)—With A, knit.
Row 2—With A, purl.
Row 3—With B, k1, * sl 2 wyib, k1, (sl 1 wyif, k1) 3 times; rep from *, end sl 2 wyib, k1.
Row 4—With B, k1, * sl 2 wyif, p7; rep from *, end sl 2 wyif, k1.
Row 5—With A, k3, * sl 1 wyif, (k1, sl 1 wyif) 3 times, k2; rep from *, end k1.
Row 6—With A, purl.
Rows 7 through 14—Repeat Rows 3 through 6 twice more.

Repeat Rows 1–14.

Woven Block Stitch

Wave and Box Stitch

This pattern and the ones that follow it are "double-ended" patterns, which means that they are not always turned at the end of a row, but sometimes there will be two consecutive rows on the right side or two consecutive rows on the wrong side. To accomplish this, it is necessary to do the knitting on *a circular needle or a pair of double-pointed needles* when working back and forth across the piece. In round knitting, of course, there is no necessity to worry about which strand is dropped on which end of the row, because at the end of a round the knitter can choose either strand to continue.

In Wave and Box Stitch, the stitches are slipped to the other end of the needle after every even-numbered or B row, so that the A strand always *follows* the B strand.

Wave and Box Stitch

Multiple of 10 sts plus 5. Colors A and B.

Row 1 (Wrong side)—With A, purl.
Row 2—With B, knit. Sl sts to other end of needle.
Row 3—With A, knit.
Row 4—With B, p1, * sl 3 wyif, p7; rep from *, end sl 3, p1. Sl sts to other end of needle.
Row 5—With A, purl.
Row 6—With B, k1, * sl 3 wyib, k7; rep from *, end sl 3, k1. Sl sts to other end of needle.
Row 7—With A, knit.
Row 8—With B, repeat Row 4. Sl sts to other end of needle.
Rows 9, 10, and 11—Repeat Rows 1, 2, and 3.
Row 12—With B, p6, * sl 3 wyif, p7; rep from *, end sl 3, p6. Sl sts to other end of needle.
Row 13—With A, purl.
Row 14—With B, k6, * sl 3 wyib, k7; rep from *, end sl 3, k6. Sl sts to other end of needle.
Row 15—With A, knit.
Row 16—With B, repeat Row 12. Sl sts to other end of needle.

Repeat Rows 1–16.

Stripe and Rib Pattern

Like all color patterns worked back and forth on double-pointed needles, this one is very easy to do in round knitting. Color B rounds are always worked like Row 2; Color A rounds are always knitted plain. The pattern geometry here is clear, formal, and sharply rectilinear, like a bold plaid.

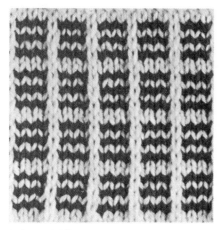

Stripe and Rib Pattern

Multiple of 4 sts plus 3. Colors A and B.

SPECIAL NOTE: This pattern must be worked back and forth on a circular needle or a pair of double-pointed needles.

Row 1 (Right side)—With A, knit.

Row 2—Sl sts to other end of needle, right side still facing, and with B, k1, * sl 1 wyib, k3; rep from *, end sl 1, k1.

Row 3—With A, purl.

Row 4—Sl sts to other end of needle, wrong side still facing, and with B, p1, * sl 1 wyif, p3; rep from *, end sl 1, p1.

Rows 5, 6, 7, and 8—Repeat Rows 1, 2, 3, and 1 again.

Row 9—With B, p1, * sl 1 wyif, p3; rep from *, end sl 1, p1.

Row 10—Sl sts to other end of needle, wrong side still facing, and with A, purl.

Row 11—With B, k1, * sl 1 wyib, k3; rep from *, end sl 1, k1.

Row 12—Sl sts to other end of needle, right side still facing, and with A, knit.

Rows 13 and 14—Repeat Rows 9 and 10.

Repeat Rows 1–14.

Reversible Two-Tone Pattern

Contributed by Bernice Haedike, Oak Park, Illinois

Reversible Two-Tone Pattern

This fascinating little knitting trick is a form of Double Knitting, which is worked on an even number of stitches as follows: * K1, sl 1 wyif; rep from * on every row. It gives two separate layers of soft stockinette stitch, connected at the edges but entirely open throughout the center like the two sides of a pocket. The difference here is that these two back-to-back layers are worked in different colors, one side in Color A, the other in Color B—and both are worked at the same time. Each color is therefore a "lining" for the other. All kinds of reversible articles can be made with this pattern; jackets, coats, scarves, baby blankets, belts.

The knitting is simple, but watch out for just two points where errors are easy to make. These points are the ends of Rows 2 and 4, when both strands are together at the same edge. Be sure always to take up the *B* strand at these two points. Color A always *follows* Color B across the rows, after the stitches are slipped to the other end of the needle. When changing colors, be sure to pick up the new strand from *under* the old one, so the two will be twisted together at the edges without leaving any holes.

The double fabric may be closed at the top by binding off all stitches in the usual way, or it may be left open, forming a pouch, by slipping all the A stitches onto one needle and all the B stitches onto another, and binding off each separately. Be generous when casting on; naturally a double-thick fabric comes out about half the width of a single thickness.

Even number of sts. Colors A and B.

NOTE: This pattern must be worked on a circular needle or a pair of double-pointed needles.

Cast on with Color A, then join Color B.

Row 1—With B, * k1, sl 1 wyif; rep from *. Sl sts to other end of needle and take up A strand.
Row 2—With A, * sl 1 wyib, p1; rep from *. Turn work and take up B strand.
Row 3—With B, * sl 1 wyib, p1; rep from *. Sl sts to other end of needle and take up A strand.
Row 4—With A, * k1, sl 1 wyif; rep from *. Turn work and take up B strand.

Repeat Rows 1–4.

Woven Plaid

A 36-row repeat is rather long for a color pattern; but in fact there are only 8 pattern rows here. On the second half (Rows 19–36) the same rows are worked on opposite sides of the fabric. The directions at the end of each row—either "turn" or "sl sts to other end of needle"—are to be considered *part of that row*. Follow these directions as soon as the row is completed, so you will not lose track of which side of the fabric you are working on. Keep the wrong-side strands *loose* when slipping each 5-stitch group.

Woven Plaid

Multiple of 10 sts plus 2. Colors A and B.

Cast on with Color A and purl one row.

SPECIAL NOTE: This pattern must be worked back and forth on a circular needle or a pair of double-pointed needles.

Row 1 (Right side)—With B, k1, * (sl 1 wyif, sl 1 wyib) twice, sl 1 wyif, k5; rep from *, end k1. Sl sts to other end of needle.
Row 2—With A, k1, * k5, sl 5 wyib; rep from *, end k1. Turn.
Row 3—With B, k1, * p5, (sl 1 wyif, sl 1 wyib) twice, sl 1 wyif; rep from *, end k1. Sl sts to other end of needle.
Row 4—With A, k1, * sl 5 wyif, p5; rep from *, end k1. Turn.
Rows 5, 6, 7, 8, and 9—Repeat Rows 1, 2, 3, 4, and Row 1 again.
Row 10—With A, k1, * k5, (sl 1 wyif, sl 1 wyib) twice, sl 1 wyif; rep from *, end k1. Turn.
Row 11—With B, k1, * p5, sl 5 wyif; rep from *, end k1. Sl sts to other end of needle.

Row 12—With A, k1, * (sl 1 wyif, sl 1 wyib) twice, sl 1 wyif, p5; rep from *, end k1. Turn.

Row 13—With B, k1, * sl 5 wyib, k5; rep from *, end k1. Sl sts to other end of needle.

Rows 14, 15, 16, 17, and 18—Repeat Rows 10, 11, 12, 13, and Row 10 again.

Row 19—With B, k1, * p5, (sl 1 wyib, sl 1 wyif) twice, sl 1 wyib; rep from *, end k1. Sl sts to other end of needle.

Row 20—With A, k1, * sl 5 wyif, p5; rep from *, end k1. Turn. (I.e., same as Row 4.)

Row 21—With B, k1, * (sl 1 wyib, sl 1 wyif) twice, sl 1 wyib, k5; rep from *, end k1. Sl sts to other end of needle.

Row 22—With A, k1, * k5, sl 5 wyib; rep from *, end k1. Turn. (I.e., same as Row 2.)

Rows 23, 24, 25, 26, and 27—Repeat Rows 19, 20, 21, 22, and Row 19 again.

Row 28—With A, k1, * (sl 1 wyib, sl 1 wyif) twice, sl 1 wyib, p5; rep from *, end k1. Turn.

Row 29—With B, k1, * sl 5 wyib, k5; rep from *, end k1. Sl sts to other end of needle. (I.e., same as Row 13.)

Row 30—With A, k1, * k5, (sl 1 wyib, sl 1 wyif) twice, sl 1 wyib; rep from *, end k1. Turn.

Row 31—With B, k1, * p5, sl 5 wyif; rep from *, end k1. Sl sts to other end of needle. (I.e., same as Row 11.)

Rows 32, 33, 34, 35, and 36—Repeat Rows 28, 29, 30, 31, and Row 28 again.

Repeat Rows 1–36.

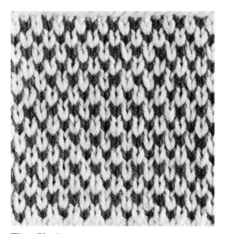

Tiny Check

Tiny Check

The little checks in this pattern are made of a single Color B stitch apiece, which means that in flat knitting the pattern must be worked back and forth on a circular needle or a pair of double-pointed needles, as given. For round knitting, as in socks, seamless sweaters, skirts, or other tubular articles, the pattern may be adapted very easily by knitting instead of purling Rows 1 and 4, and slipping sts wyib instead of wyif in Row 4. The "sl sts to other end of needle" direction can be ignored, since at the end of a round either strand may be picked up at will.

Odd number of sts. Colors A and B.

SPECIAL NOTE: This pattern must be worked back and forth on a circular needle or a pair of double-pointed needles.

Row 1 (Wrong side)—With A, purl.

Row 2—With B, k1, * sl 1 wyib, k1; rep from *.

Row 3—Sl all sts to other end of needle and with A, knit.

Row 4—With B, p2, * sl 1 wyif, p1; rep from *, end p1. Sl all sts to other end of needle.

Repeat Rows 1–4.

Woven Polka Dot Pattern

This is an "easy" version of Swedish Weave; it is simplified because the yarns are handled one at a time, instead of both together. The principle remains the same, however; Color B is never worked, only woven: in this case, twice for each "dot", so that there is a double strand showing instead of a single one. The single purl stitch at the beginning of Rows 4 and 8 anchors Color B at the left-hand edge. On the right-hand edge it is automatically caught as the strands are twisted up the side. With this pattern it is especially important always to pick up a new strand from *behind* the old one when changing colors.

A three-color version of the pattern might be worked with a Color C introduced in Rows 7 and 8.

Woven Polka Dot Pattern

Odd number of sts. Colors A and B.

Row 1 (Right side)—With A, knit.
Row 2—With A, k1, purl to last st, k1.
Row 3—With B, * sl 1 wyib, sl 1 wyif; rep from *, end sl 1 wyib. (No sts are knitted in Color B; the strand is simply woven through the Color A sts.)
Row 4—With B, p1, * sl 1 wyib, sl 1 wyif; rep from *.
Rows 5 and 6—With A, repeat Rows 1 and 2.
Row 7—With B, * sl 1 wyif, sl 1 wyib; rep from *, end sl 1 wyif.
Row 8—With B, carry yarn around side edge of work and p1, * sl 1 wyif, sl 1 wyib; rep from *.

Repeat Rows 1–8.

Two-Color Bind Stitch

Work this pattern with a light hand, being careful not to bind the stitches too tightly. "Squeezing" will spoil its appearance. The wrapped strands should be soft and reasonably loose, though not slack. The pattern is pretty, too, in three colors. Simply alternate the three colors continuously, giving 4 rows to each in turn.

Multiple of 4 sts plus 2. Colors A and B.

Cast on with Color A and purl one row.

Row 1 (Right side)—With B, k1, * sl 2 wyif, put yarn to back and sl the same 2 sts back to left-hand needle, bring yarn to front and sl the same 2 sts wyif again, put yarn to back and k2; rep from *, end k1.
Row 2—With B, p3, * sl 2 wyif, p2; rep from *, end sl 2, p1.
Row 3—With B, k3, * p2, k2; rep from *, end p2, k1.
Row 4—With B, purl.

ABOVE: *Two-Color Bind Stitch*
BELOW: *Swedish Dot Pattern*

Row 5—With A, k3, rep from * of Row 1; end last repeat k1 instead of k2.
Row 6—With A, p1, * sl 2 wyif, p2; rep from *, end p1.
Row 7—With A, k1, * p2, k2; rep from *, end k1.
Row 8—With A, purl.

Repeat Rows 1–8.

Swedish Dot Pattern

This charming and simple little pattern is easy to knit in color-reversal stripes, as follows: work Rows 1 through 10 as given. Then work Rows 1 through 4 in Color B, Rows 11 and 12 in Color A, and Rows 1 through 4 in Color B; then begin again at Row 1 with A. This will give dark stripes with light dots, alternating with light stripes with dark dots.

Multiple of 4 sts plus 2. Colors A and B.

Rows 1 and 3 (Right side)—With A, knit.
Rows 2 and 4—With A, purl.
Row 5—With B, k3, * sl 2 wyif, k2; rep from *, end sl 2, k1.
Row 6—With B, k1, * sl 2 wyif, k2; rep from *, end k1.
Rows 7, 8, 9, and 10—With A, repeat Rows 1, 2, 3, and 4.
Row 11—With B, repeat Row 6.
Row 12—With B, repeat Row 5.

Repeat Rows 1–12.

Salt and Pepper Tweed
ABOVE: *right side*
BELOW: *wrong side*

Salt and Pepper Tweed

This attractive variation on a two-color Fabric Stitch can be used either way round. The right side is a tweedy mixture; the wrong side shows a series of narrow horizontal stripes. This pattern closes up into a thick, dense fabric, and should be worked with large needles. More than two colors can be used, if desired; simply repeat the same two pattern rows for each color.

Even number of sts. Colors A and B.

Cast on with Color A.

Row 1 (Right side)—With B, * k1, sl 1 wyib; rep from *.
Row 2—With B, * k1, sl 1 wyif; rep from *.
Rows 3 and 4—With A, repeat Rows 1 and 2.

Repeat Rows 1–4.

Four-Color Mix   *See color page iii*

This pattern is a real mixture. Single stitches of each of the four colors chase each other all over the fabric in rich profusion. All sorts of subtle heathery or tweedy effects are possible with this pattern, depending on how your chosen colors blend or contrast with each other.

Multiple of 4 sts plus 3. Colors A, B, C, and D.

Cast on with Color A and purl one row.

Row 1 (Right side)—With B, k1, * sl 1 wyib, k3; rep from *, end sl 1, k1.
Row 2—With C, p3, * sl 1 wyif, p3; rep from *.
Row 3—With D, repeat Row 1.
Row 4—With B, repeat Row 2.
Row 5—With A, repeat Row 1.
Row 6—With D, repeat Row 2.
Row 7—With C, repeat Row 1.
Row 8—With A, repeat Row 2.

Repeat Rows 1–8.

Sherwood Pattern   *See color page iii*

This is a simple three-and-one pattern having only eight rows in fact; but in the alternation of colors these 8 rows are repeated 3 times. This makes a fabric with a very pleasing and subtle design that seems more complicated than it really is.

Multiple of 4 sts plus 3. Colors A, B, and C.

Row 1 (Right side)—With A, knit.
Row 2—With A, purl.
Row 3—With B, k3, * sl 1 wyib, k3; rep from *.
Row 4—With B, k3, * sl 1 wyif, k3; rep from *.
Row 5—With C, k1, * sl 1 wyib, k3; rep from *, end sl 1, k1.
Row 6—With C, k1, * sl 1 wyif, k3; rep from *, end sl 1, k1.
Row 7—With A, repeat Row 3.
Row 8—With A, p1, k1, p1, * sl 1 wyif, p1, k1, p1; rep from *.
Rows 9 and 10—With B, repeat Rows 1 and 2.
Rows 11 and 12—With C, repeat Rows 3 and 4.
Rows 13 and 14—With A, repeat Rows 5 and 6.
Rows 15 and 16—With B, repeat Rows 7 and 8.
Rows 17 and 18—With C, repeat Rows 1 and 2.
Rows 19 and 20—With A, repeat Rows 3 and 4.
Rows 21 and 22—With B, repeat Rows 5 and 6.
Rows 23 and 24—With C, repeat Rows 7 and 8.

Repeat Rows 1–24.

Dice Check *See color page iv*

Like most of the really ingenious patterns in knitting, this one is created by a small—almost insignificant—change in a commonly known technique. Here, an ordinary two-stitch check is transformed by the simple expedient of carrying a third color back and forth, one row at a time. This enables the knitter to work an elegant, tidy three-color check without breaking any of the three strands. The pattern is so easy to work that a beginner may use it to make a beautiful coat, casual dress, sweater, mittens or baby clothes.

Multiple of 4 sts plus 2. Colors A, B, and C.

Row 1 (Wrong side)—With A, purl.
Row 2—With B, k1, sl 1 wyib, * k2, sl 2 wyib; rep from *, end k2, sl 1, k1.
Row 3—With B, p1, sl 1 wyif, * p2, sl 2 wyif; rep from *, end p2, sl 1, p1.
Row 4—With A, knit.
Row 5—With C, p2, * sl 2 wyif, p2; rep from *.
Row 6—With C, k2, * sl 2 wyib, k2; rep from *.

Repeat Rows 1–6.

Syncopated Tweed *See color page iv*

This beautiful tweed is so simple as to be well within the reach of any beginner; yet the finished fabric seems to be quite a complex arrangement of color spots. It is a dense fabric that tends to curl forward, because of the pull of the long slip-stitches, and so it requires pressing.

Multiple of 3 sts plus 2. Colors A, B, and C.

Row 1 (Right side)—With A, knit.
Row 2—With A, k1, * sl 1 wyif, p2; rep from *, end k1.
Row 3—With B, k3, * sl 1 wyib, k2; rep from *, end sl 1, k1.
Row 4—With B, repeat Row 2.
Row 5—With C, knit.
Row 6—With C, k1, p1, * sl 1 wyif, p2; rep from *, end sl 1, p1, k1.
Row 7—With A, k2, * sl 1 wyib, k2; rep from *.
Row 8—With A, repeat Row 6.
Row 9—With B, knit.
Row 10—With B, k1, * p2, sl 1 wyif; rep from *, end k1.
Row 11—With C, k1, * sl 1 wyib, k2; rep from *, end k1.
Row 12—With C, repeat Row 10.

Repeat Rows 1–12.

Barred Stripes

Here is a simple and attractive pattern of the "ladder" type, making a nice firm fabric for ski sweaters and other outdoor wear. The wrong side shows the same pattern in purl stitches.

Multiple of 4 sts plus 2. Colors A and B.

Cast on with A and purl one row.

Row 1 (Right side)—With B, k1, * sl 2 wyif, k2; rep from *, end k1.

Row 2—With B, k1, * p2, sl 2 wyif; rep from *, end k1.

Row 3—With A, k3, * sl 2 wyif, k2; rep from *, end sl 2 wyif, k1.

Row 4—With A, k1, * sl 2 wyif, p2; rep from *, end k1.

Repeat Rows 1–4.

Barred Stripes

Bold Check Pattern

This is a big, striking check suitable for sport coats, sweaters and blankets.

Multiple of 10 sts plus 2. Colors A and B.

Row 1 (Right side)—With A, knit.

Row 2—With A, (k1, p1) twice, k1, * p2, k1, p1, k1; rep from *, end p2, (k1, p1) twice, k1.

Row 3—With B, k1, * k5, (sl 1 wyib, k1) twice, sl 1 wyib; rep from *, end k1.

Row 4—With B, k1, * (sl 1 wyif, k1) twice, sl 1 wyif, k5; rep from *, end k1.

Row 5—With A, k2, * sl 1 wyib, k1, sl 1 wyib, k7; rep from *.

Row 6—With A, * (k1, p1) 3 times, (k1, sl 1 wyif) twice; rep from *, end k2.

Rows 7, 8, 9, 10, 11, and 12—Repeat Rows 3, 4, 5, and 6, then Rows 3 and 4 again.

Rows 13 and 14—With A, repeat Rows 1 and 2.

Row 15—With B, k1, * (sl 1 wyib, k1) twice, sl 1 wyib, k5; rep from *, end k1.

Row 16—With B, k1, * k5, (sl 1 wyif, k1) twice, sl 1 wyif; rep from *, end k1.

Row 17—With A, * k7, sl 1 wyib, k1, sl 1 wyib; rep from *, end k2.

Row 18—With A, k2, * (sl 1 wyif, k1) twice, (p1, k1) 3 times; rep from *.

Rows 19, 20, 21, 22, 23, and 24—Repeat Rows 15, 16, 17, and 18, then Rows 15 and 16 again.

Repeat Rows 1–24.

ABOVE: *Bold Check Pattern*
BELOW: *Garter-Stitch Stripe Version*

GARTER-STITCH STRIPE VERSION

Work the same as Bold Check Pattern above, with the following exceptions:

Rows 5, 9, 17, and 21—With A, knit.

Rows 6 and 10—With A, k1, * (p1, k1) twice, p1, k5; rep from *, end k1.

Rows 18 and 22—With A, k1, * k5, (p1, k1) twice, p1; rep from *, end k1.

Tuscan Pattern

Here is a delightful pattern of big checks in contrasting garter-stitch and woven-stitch textures, for beautiful tweedy coats and jackets.

Multiple of 10 sts plus 9. Colors A and B.

Cast on with Color A and purl one row.

Row 1 (Right side)—With B, k2, * (sl 1 wyif, k1) twice, sl 1 wyif, k5; rep from *, end last repeat k2.

Row 2—With B, repeat Row 1.

Row 3—With A, k1, * (sl 1 wyif, k1) 3 times, sl 1 wyif, k3; rep from *, end last repeat k1.

Row 4—With A, k1, * (sl 1 wyif, p1) 3 times, sl 1 wyif, k3; rep from *, end last repeat k1.

Rows 5 through 14—Repeat Rows 1 through 4 twice more, then Rows 1 and 2 again.

Row 15—With A, k3, * sl 1 wyif, k1, sl 1 wyif, k7; rep from *, end last repeat k3.

Row 16—With A, p3, * sl 1 wyif, p1, sl 1 wyif, p7; rep from *, end last repeat p3.

Rows 17 and 18—With B, k1, sl 1 wyif, * k5, (sl 1 wyif, k1) twice, sl 1 wyif; rep from *, end k5, sl 1 wyif, k1.

Row 19—With A, k2, sl 1 wyif, * k3, (sl 1 wyif, k1) 3 times, sl 1 wyif; rep from *, end k3, sl 1 wyif, k2.

Row 20—With A, k1, p1, sl 1 wyif, *k3, (sl 1 wyif, p1) 3 times, sl 1 wyif; rep from *, end k3, sl 1 wyif, p1, k1.

Rows 21 through 30—Repeat Rows 17 through 20 twice more, then Rows 17 and 18 again.

Row 31—With A, k8, * sl 1 wyif, k1, sl 1 wyif, k7; rep from *, end k1.

Row 32—With A, p8, * sl 1 wyif, p1, sl 1 wyif, p7; rep from *, end p1.

Repeat Rows 1–32.

Tuscan Pattern

Sandwich Stitch

A simple variation on a garter-stitch stripe is seen here, which makes a sporty check for children's sweaters, jackets and coats. Recommended for beginning knitters.

Multiple of 16 sts plus 9. Colors A and B.

NOTE: Odd-numbered rows are right-side rows.

Rows 1, 2, 5, 6, 9, 10, 13, and 14—With A, knit.

Rows 3 and 7—With B, (k1, sl 1 wyib) 4 times, * k9, (sl 1 wyib, k1) 3 times, sl 1 wyib; rep from *, end k1.

Rows 4 and 8—With B, (k1, sl 1 wyif) 4 times, * p9, (sl 1 wyif, k1) 3 times, sl 1 wyif; rep from *, end k1.

Rows 11 and 15—With B, k9, * (sl 1 wyib, k1) 3 times, sl 1 wyib, k9; rep from *.

Rows 12 and 16—With B, p9, * (sl 1 wyif, k1) 3 times, sl 1 wyif, p9; rep from *.

Repeat Rows 1–16.

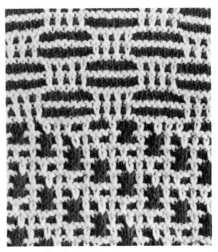

ABOVE: *Sandwich Stitch*
BELOW: *Watergate Pattern*

Watergate Pattern

Like Sandwich Stitch, this pattern has a garter-stitch-stripe basis, but is a little more complicated. Certain background stitches are carried up over the stripes to make motifs that "travel" on a shallow diagonal.

Multiple of 20 sts plus 3. Colors A and B.

NOTE: On all odd-numbered (right-side) rows, sl all sl-sts wyib. On all even-numbered (wrong-side) rows, sl all sl-sts wyif. Cast on with A and knit one row.

Row 1 (Right side)—With B, k1, * sl 1, k2, (sl 1, k1) twice, sl 1, k2, (sl 1, k4) twice; rep from *, end sl 1, k1.

Rows 2, 6, 10, and 14—With B, purl all the sts knitted on previous row, slipping all sl-sts wyif.

Row 3—With A, * k13, sl 2, k3, sl 2; rep from *, end k3.

Row 4—With A, k3, * sl 2, k3, p2, k13; rep from *.

Row 5—With B, k1, * sl 1, k4, sl 1, k2, (sl 1, k1) twice, sl 1, k2, sl 1, k4; rep from *, end sl 1, k1.

Row 7—With A, k3, * sl 2, k13, sl 2, k3; rep from*.

Row 8—With A, k3, * p2, k13, sl 2, k3; rep from * .

Row 9—With B, k1, * (sl 1, k4) twice, sl 1, k2, (sl 1, k1) twice, sl 1, k2; rep from *, end sl 1, k1.

Row 11—With A, k3, * sl 2, k3, sl 2, k13; rep from *.

Row 12—With A, * k13, sl 2, k3, p2; rep from *, end k3.

Row 13—With B, * (k1, sl 1) twice, k2, sl 1, (k4, sl 1) twice, k2, sl 1; rep from *, end k1, sl 1, k1.

Row 15—With A, k8, * sl 2, k3, sl 2, k13; rep from *, end last repeat k8.

Row 16—With A, k8, * sl 2, k3, p2, k13; rep from *, end last repeat k8.

Repeat Rows 1–16.

Winged Wave Pattern

Winged Wave Pattern

This charming fabric is thick, warm, non-curling, and beautiful in all types of sportswear. The pattern is easy to work, although the main pattern row (Row 6) seems complicated in the directions; but the technique is soon learned, and is worked in much less time than it takes to tell about it.

Multiple of 8 sts plus 2. Colors A and B.

PREPARATION ROWS:

Row 1 (Wrong side)—With A, k4, * p2 wrapping yarn twice for each st, k6; rep from *, end last repeat k4.

Row 2—With B, k4, * sl 2 wyib dropping extra wraps, k6; rep from *, end last repeat k4.

End of Preparation Rows.

Row 3—With B, k4, * sl 2 wyif, k6; rep from *, end last repeat k4.

Row 4—With B, k4, * sl 2 wyib, k6; rep from *, end last repeat k4.

Row 5—With B, k3, * p1 wrapping yarn twice, sl 2 wyif, p1 wrapping yarn twice, k4; rep from *, end last repeat k3.

Row 6—With A, k1, * sl 3 wyib dropping extra wrap from 3rd st; drop first elongated Color A st off needle to front of work, sl the same 3 sts back to left-hand needle, pick up dropped st and knit it; then k2, sl 1 wyib, drop second elongated Color A st off needle to front of work, sl 3 wyib dropping extra wrap from 1st st, pick up dropped st and place it on left-hand needle, then sl *two* (the 2nd and 3rd) of the 3 slipped sts back to left-hand needle, then k3; rep from *, end k1.

Rows 7, 8, 9, and 10—Repeat Rows 3, 4, 5, and 6, reversing colors (i.e., A, A, A, B).

Omit Rows 1 and 2, repeat Rows 3–10.

Holiday Stripes

A drop-stitch technique is used in this stripe pattern, which combines all the best elements of pattern knitting. It is highly ingenious in concept and execution; it is strikingly novel in effect; and it is exceedingly simple to work. If you look carefully, you will see little slip-stitch "cables" embedded in the fabric. These can be brought out, if desired, by working in a single solid color with purl stitches, instead of knit stitches, inserted between them (i.e., on right-side rows purl the first stitch and every 4th stitch thereafter). But in two-color knitting, the "cables" form the rick-rack-like stripes and thus do not exist as vertical patterns.

Holiday Stripes

Multiple of 4 sts plus 2. Colors A and B.

Row 1 (Wrong side)—With A, purl.
Row 2—With B, * k1, sl 1 wyib; rep from *, end k2.
Row 3—With B, p4, * sl 1 wyif, p3; rep from *, end sl 1, p1.
Row 4—With B, * k1, drop sl-st off needle to front of work, k2, pick up dropped st and knit it ; rep from *, end k2.
Row 5—With B, purl.
Rows 6, 7, and 8—With A, repeat Rows 2, 3, and 4.

Repeat Rows 1–8.

Petal Quilting

Multiple of 8 sts plus 1. Colors A and B.

Row 1 (Right side)—With A, knit.
Row 2—With A, k1, * p1 wrapping yarn twice, k5, p1 wrapping yarn twice, k1; rep from *.
Row 3—With B, k1, * sl 1 wyib dropping extra wrap, k5, sl 1 wyib dropping extra wrap, k1; rep from *.
Rows 4 and 6—With B, p1, * sl 1 wyif, p5, sl 1 wyif, p1; rep from *.
Row 5—With B, k1, * sl 1 wyib, k5, sl 1 wyib, k1; rep from *.
Row 7—With A, k1, * drop Color A sl-st off needle to front of work, k2, pick up dropped st and knit it; k1, sl 2 wyib, drop next Color A sl-st off needle, sl the same 2 sts back to left-hand needle, pick up dropped st and knit it; k2, sl 1 wyib; rep from *, end last repeat k1 instead of sl 1.

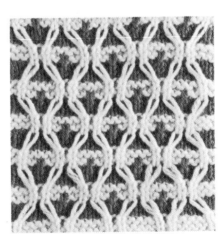

Petal Quilting

Row 8—With A, k3, * p1, k1, p1, k2, sl 1 wyif, k2; rep from *, end p1, k1, p1, k3.

Row 9—With A, knit.

Row 10—With A, k3, * p1 wrapping yarn twice, k1, p1 wrapping yarn twice, k5; rep from *, end last repeat k3.

Row 11—With B, k3, * sl 1 wyib dropping extra wrap, k1, sl 1 wyib dropping extra wrap, k5; rep from *, end last repeat k3.

Rows 12 and 14—With B, p3, * sl 1 wyif, p1, sl 1 wyif, p5; rep from *, end last repeat p3.

Row 13—With B, k3, * sl 1 wyib, k1, sl 1 wyib, k5; rep from *, end last repeat k3.

Row 15—With A, k1, * sl 2 wyib, drop Color A sl-st off needle to front of work, sl the same 2 sts back to left-hand needle, pick up dropped st and knit it; k2, sl 1 wyib, drop next Color A sl-st off needle, k2, pick up dropped st and knit it, k1; rep from *.

Row 16—With A, k1, * p1, k2, sl 1 wyif, k2, p1, k1; rep from *.

Repeat Rows 1–16.

Surprise Pattern in three colors

Surprise Pattern in two colors

Surprise Pattern

The "surprise" is the way this pattern looks when it is worked in only two colors instead of three. The shapes are entirely different. For the two-color version, simply alternate colors every other row, as follows: Rows 1, 4, 5, 8, 9, and 12 in Color A; Rows 2, 3, 6, 7, 10, and 11 in Color B.

Multiple of 4 sts plus 1. Colors A, B, and C.

Row 1 (Wrong side)—With A, purl.

Row 2—With B, k2, * sl 1 wyib, k3; rep from *, end sl 1, k2.

Row 3—With B, p2, * sl 1 wyif, p3; rep from *, end sl 1, p2.

Row 4—With C, k4, * sl 1 wyib, k3; rep from *, end k1.

Row 5—With C, p4, * sl 1 wyif, p3; rep from *, end p1.

Row 6—With A, k1, * sl 1 wyib, k1; rep from *.

Row 7—With A, purl.

Row 8—With B, k2, * sl 1 wyib, k1; rep from *, end k1.

Row 9—With B, p4, * sl 1 wyif, p3; rep from *, end p1.

Row 10—With C, k2, * sl 1 wyib, k3; rep from *, end sl 1, k2.

Row 11—With C, purl.

Row 12—With A, k1, * sl 1 wyib, k1; rep from *.

Repeat Rows 1–12.

Outlined Check Pattern   *See color page v*

This pretty four-color design is worked from both edges at once. Color A is always left at the right-hand edge, Colors C and D are always left at the left-hand edge, and Color B travels back and forth to connect them.

Multiple of 10 sts plus 4.

Colors A, B, C, and D.

Row 1 (Right side)—With A, knit.
Row 2—With A, purl.
Row 3—With B, k1, * sl 2 wyib, k8; rep from *, end sl 2, k1.
Row 4—With C, p1, sl 3 wyif, * p6, sl 4 wyif; rep from *, end p6, sl 3, p1.
Row 5—With C, k1, sl 3 wyib, * k6, sl 4 wyib; rep from *, end k6, sl 3, k1.
Row 6—With B, p1, * sl 2 wyif, p8; rep from *, end sl 2, p1.
Rows 7 and 8—With A, repeat Rows 1 and 2.
Row 9—With B, k6, * sl 2 wyib, k8; rep from *, end sl 2, k6.
Row 10—With D, p5, * sl 4 wyif, p6; rep from *, end sl 4, p5.
Row 11—With D, k5, * sl 4 wyib, k6; rep from *, end sl 4, k5.
Row 12—With B, p6, * sl 2 wyif, p8; rep from *, end sl 2, p6.

Repeat Rows 1–12.

Haystack Stripe   *See color page v*

This is a gay and interesting pattern of only eight rows, which are repeated three times in order to alternate the colors. At first glance it appears to be a design of horizontal stripes, which are elongated upward and downward at intervals. But look more closely, and you will see that it is really a pattern of slip-cross cables, worked continuously across the fabric with a half-drop. This true design immediately becomes apparent if the pattern is worked in one solid color, using the basic eight rows only.

Multiple of 6 sts plus 2. Colors A, B, and C.

Cast on with Color A and knit one row.

Row 1 (Wrong side)—With A, k1, * p1 wrapping yarn twice, p1, p1 wrapping yarn twice, p3; rep from *, end k1.
Row 2—With B, k4, * sl 1 wyib dropping extra wrap, k1, sl 1 wyib dropping extra wrap, k3; rep from *, end last repeat k1 instead of k3.
Row 3—With B, k1, * sl 1 wyif, p1, sl 1 wyif, p3; rep from *, end k1.
Row 4—With B, k4, * drop next st off needle to front of work, sl 1 wyib, drop next st off needle to front of work; then with left-hand needle pick up *first* dropped st,

sl the same center st from right-hand needle back to left-hand needle, then pick up *second* dropped st and replace it on left-hand needle; then k6 (the 3 sts just crossed, and the following 3); rep from *, end last repeat k4 instead of k6.

Row 5—With B, k1, * p3, p1 wrapping yarn twice, p1, p1 wrapping yarn twice; rep from *, end k1.

Row 6—With C, k1, * sl 1 wyib dropping extra wrap, k1, sl 1 wyib dropping extra wrap, k3; rep from *, end k1.

Row 7—With C, k1, * p3, sl 1 wyif, p1, sl 1 wyif; rep from *, end k1.

Row 8—With C, k1, rep from * of Row 4 across to last st, end k1.

Row 9—With C, repeat Row 1.

Rows 10, 11, 12, and 13—With A, repeat Rows 2, 3, 4, and 5.

Rows 14, 15, 16, and 17—With B, repeat Rows 6, 7, 8, and 1.

Rows 18, 19, 20, and 21—With C, repeat Rows 2, 3, 4, and 5.

Rows 22, 23, and 24—With A, repeat Rows 6, 7, and 8.

Repeat Rows 1–24.

Four-Color Progressive Tweed

See color page vi

This pattern is so named because it "progresses" from right to left; each succeeding spot of the same color is moved two stitches over from its previous position. Try it in four gently-shading colors, such as cream, beige, gold and brown; or try it in four wildly contrasting ones—white, orange, emerald and black, for instance. The effect is very pleasing either way.

Multiple of 6 sts plus 2. Colors A, B, C, and D.

Cast on with Color A and purl one row.

Row 1 (Right side)—With B, k1, * sl 2 wyib, k4; rep from *, end k1.

Row 2—With B, k1, * k2, p2, sl 2 wyif; rep from *, end k1.

Row 3—With C, k3, * sl 2 wyib, k4; rep from *, end sl 2, k3.

Row 4—With C, k1, * p2, sl 2 wyif, k2; rep from *, end k1.

Row 5—With D, k1, * k4, sl 2 wyib; rep from *, end k1.

Row 6—With D, k1, * sl 2 wyif, k2, p2; rep from *, end k1.

Rows 7 and 8—With A, repeat Rows 1 and 2.

Rows 9 and 10—With B, repeat Rows 3 and 4.

Rows 11 and 12—With C, repeat Rows 5 and 6.

Rows 13 and 14—With D, repeat Rows 1 and 2.

Rows 15 and 16—With A, repeat Rows 3 and 4.

Rows 17 and 18—With B, repeat Rows 5 and 6.

Rows 19 and 20—With C, repeat Rows 1 and 2.

Rows 21 and 22—With D, repeat Rows 3 and 4.

Rows 23 and 24—With A, repeat Rows 5 and 6.

Repeat Rows 1–24.

Corn on the Cob Stitch

This fabric, knitted in narrow vertical stripes, is nubby and very dense. It is well suited to heavy knitted coats and jackets calculated to keep the wind out; and it can be done also in fine yarn for such articles as gloves.

Even number of sts. Colors A and B.

Cast on with Color A and knit one row.

Row 1 (Right side)—With B, k1, * k1, sl 1 wyib; rep from *, end k1.
Row 2—With B, k1, * sl 1 wyif, k1; rep from *, end k1.
Row 3—With A, k1, * sl 1 wyib, k1-b; rep from *, end k1.
Row 4—With A, k1, * k1, sl 1 wyif; rep from *, end k1.

Repeat Rows 1–4.

VARIATION: *PIN STRIPE PATTERN*

Work Pin Stripe Pattern the same as Corn on the Cob Stitch, except in Rows 2 and 4 *purl* instead of knit.

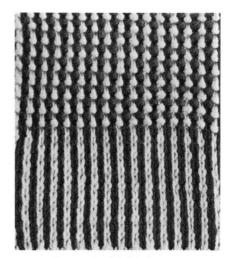

ABOVE: *Corn on the Cob Stitch*
BELOW: *Pin Stripe Pattern*

Waffle Check

This pattern is the same as Pin Check, except that it has a garter-stitch basis which lends it a nubby texture.

Odd number of sts. Colors A and B.

Row 1 (Wrong side)—With A, knit.
Row 2—With B, k1, * sl 1 wyib, k1; rep from *.
Row 3—With B, k1, * sl 1 wyif, k1; rep from *.
Rows 4 and 5—With A, knit.
Row 6—With B, k2, * sl 1 wyib, k1; rep from *, end k1.
Row 7—With B, k2, * sl 1 wyif, k1; rep from *, end k1.
Row 8—With A, knit.

Repeat Rows 1–8.

WAFFLE CHECK VARIATION

To align the checks vertically instead of alternating them, repeat Rows 1–4 only.

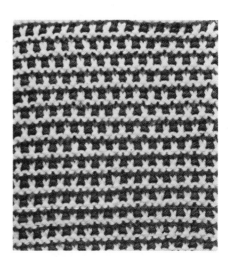

ABOVE: *Waffle Check*
BELOW: *Variation*

Pin Check

This pattern is identical with Waffle Check except for Rows 1 and 5. Yet this small difference gives quite a different texture.

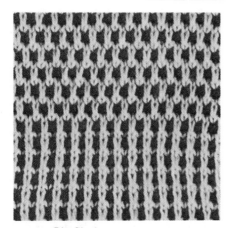

ABOVE: *Pin Check*
BELOW: *Variation*

Odd number of sts. Colors A and B.

Row 1 (Wrong side)—With A, purl.
Row 2—With B, k1, * sl 1 wyib, k1; rep from *.
Row 3—With B, k1, * sl 1 wyif, k1; rep from *.
Row 4—With A, knit.
Row 5—With A, purl.
Row 6—With B, k2, * sl 1 wyib, k1; rep from *, end k1.
Row 7—With B, k2, * sl 1 wyif, k1; rep from *, end k1.
Row 8—With A, knit.

Repeat Rows 1–8.

PIN CHECK VARIATION

Repeat Rows 1–4 only. In this way the checks are aligned vertically above one another instead of being alternated.

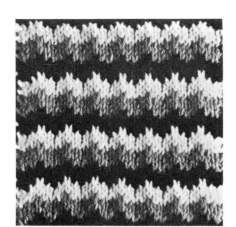

Tricolor Wave Stripes

Tricolor Wave Stripes

Multiple of 4 sts plus 1. Colors A, B, and C.

Cast on with Color A and purl one row.

Row 1 (Right side)—With B, k1, * sl 3 wyib, k1; rep from *.
Row 2—With B, p2, * sl 1 wyif, p3; rep from *, end sl 1, p2.
Row 3—With B, knit.
Row 4—With B, purl.
Rows 5–8—With C, repeat Rows 1–4.
Rows 9–12—With A, repeat Rows 1–4.

Repeat Rows 1–12.

Ripple Stripes

Ripple Stripes

This is a smaller version of Tricolor Wave Stripes.

Multiple of 4 sts plus 2. Colors A and B.

Rows 1 and 3 (Right side)—With A, knit.
Rows 2 and 4—With A, purl.
Row 5—With B, k2, * sl 2 wyib, k2; rep from *.
Row 6—With B, purl.
Row 7—With A, repeat Row 5.
Row 8—With A, purl.

Repeat Rows 1–8.

Dotted Ladder Pattern

In this pretty vertical-stripe variation, each stripe contains accents of its opposite color, which makes the overall effect more interesting than plain vertical stripes.

Multiple of 6 sts plus 5. Colors A and B.

Cast on with Color A and purl one row.

Row 1 (Right side)—With B, k1, * sl 1 wyib, k1, sl 1 wyib, k3; rep from *, end last repeat k1.
Row 2—With B, k1, * sl 1 wyif, k1, sl 1 wyif, p3; rep from * to last 4 sts, end (sl 1 wyif, k1) twice.
Row 3—With A, k1, * k3, sl 1 wyib, k1, sl 1 wyib; rep from * to last 4 sts, end k4.
Row 4—With A, k1, * p3, sl 1 wyif, k1, sl 1 wyif; rep from *, end p3, k1.

Repeat Rows 1–4.

Dotted Ladder Pattern

Stripe and Spot Pattern

This is another traditional French pattern which has innumerable variations. Colors A and B may be carried up the side of the piece, but it is better to break off Color C at the end of Row 8 and re-join it at the next repeat.

Odd number of sts. Colors A, B, and C.

Rows 1 and 3 (Right side)—With A, knit.
Rows 2 and 4—With A, purl.
Rows 5 and 6—With B, knit.
Row 7—With C, k1, * sl 1 wyib, k1; rep from *.
Row 8—With C, k1, * sl 1 wyif, k1; rep from *.
Rows 9 and 10—With B, knit.
Row 11—With A, k2, * sl 1 wyib, k1; rep from *, end k1.
Row 12—With A, p2, * sl 1 wyif, p1; rep from *, end p1.

Repeat Rows 1–12.

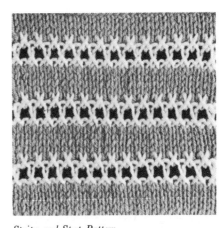

Stripe and Spot Pattern

Tricolor Fabric Stitch

This is one of the most fascinating of three-color patterns, adaptable to dozens of useful and decorative knitted articles. It must be worked on fairly large needles.

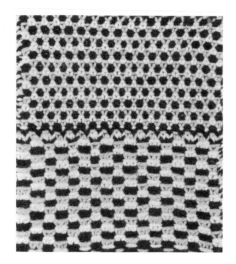

Odd number of sts. Colors A, B, and C.

Cast on with Color A and purl one row.

Row 1 (Right side)—With B, k1, * sl 1 wyif, k1; rep from *.
Row 2—With C, k1, p1, * sl 1 wyib, p1; rep from *, end k1.
Row 3—With A, repeat Row 1.
Row 4—With B, repeat Row 2.
Row 5—With C, repeat Row 1.
Row 6—With A, repeat Row 2.

Repeat Rows 1–6.

ABOVE: *Tricolor Fabric Stitch*
BELOW: *Double Tricolor Fabric Stitch*

Double Tricolor Fabric Stitch

Multiple of 4 sts. Colors A, B, and C.

Cast on with Color A and purl one row.

Row 1 (Right side)—With B, k1, * sl 2 wyif, k2; rep from *, end sl 2 wyif, k1.
Row 2—With C, k1, p2, * sl 2 wyib, p2; rep from *, end k1.
Row 3—With A, repeat Row 1.
Row 4—With B, repeat Row 2.
Row 5—With C, repeat Row 1.
Row 6—With A, repeat Row 2.

Repeat Rows 1–6.

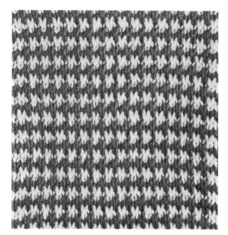

Honeycomb Tweed

Honeycomb Tweed

There seems little reason to give this pattern the name of "Honeycomb"—there are far too many different Honeycombs in knitted patterns already—but nevertheless, this tweed pattern makes one more. It is a most adaptable pattern, of French origin.

Odd number of sts. Colors A and B.

Cast on with Color A.

Row 1 (Right side)—With B, k1, * sl 1 wyib, k1; rep from *.
Row 2—With B, purl.
Row 3—With A, k2, * sl 1 wyib, k1; rep from *, end k1.
Row 4—With A, purl.

Repeat Rows 1–4.

Striped Check Pattern *See color page vii*

This French pattern makes a beautiful and simple-to-work four-color tweed.

Multiple of 4 sts plus 3. Colors A, B, C, and D.

Cast on with Color D.

Row 1 (Right side)—With A, k1, * sl 1 wyib, k3; rep from *, end sl 1, k1.
Row 2—With A, p1, * sl 1 wyif, p3; rep from *, end sl 1, p1.
Row 3—With B, * k3, sl 1 wyib; rep from *, end k3.
Row 4—With B, * p3, sl 1 wyif; rep from *, end p3.
Rows 5 and 6—With C, repeat Rows 1 and 2.
Rows 7 and 8—With D, repeat Rows 3 and 4.

Repeat Rows 1–8.

Four-Color Fancy Pattern *See color page vii*

This is a very pleasing pattern for ski sweaters, mittens, and hats. It is gay, colorful, and a lot simpler than it looks.

Multiple of 4 sts plus 3. Colors A, B, C, and D.

Cast on with Color A.

NOTE: On all even-numbered rows, all slip-stitches are slipped with yarn in back. On all odd-numbered rows, all slip-stitches are slipped with yarn in front.

Row 1 (Wrong side)—With A, k1, purl to last st, k1.
Row 2—With B, k2, * sl 1, k1; rep from *, end k1.
Row 3—With B, k1, p1, * sl 1, p1; rep from *, end k1.
Row 4—With C, k1, * sl 1, k1; rep from *.
Row 5—With C, k1, purl to last st, k1.
Row 6—With D, k1, * sl 1, k3; rep from *, end sl 1, k1.
Row 7—With D, k1, * sl 1, p3; rep from *, end sl 1, k1.
Row 8—With B, k2, * sl 3, k1; rep from *, end k1.
Row 9—With B, k1, p2, * sl 1, p3; rep from *, end sl 1, p2, k1.
Row 10—With A, repeat Row 6.

Repeat Rows 1–10.

Triangle Check

Triangle Check

NOTE: On all right-side rows (odd numbers) sl all sl-sts with yarn in back; on all wrong-side rows (even numbers) sl all sl-sts with yarn in front.

Multiple of 6 sts plus 3. Colors A and B.

Cast on with Color B and purl one row.

Row 1 (Right side)—With A, k1, * sl 1, k5; rep from *, end sl 1, k1.
Row 2—With A, k1, * sl 1, p5; rep from *, end sl 1, k1.
Row 3—With B, k3, * sl 3, k3; rep from *.
Row 4—With B, k1, p2, * sl 3, p3; rep from *, end sl 3, p2, k1.
Row 5—With A, k1, sl 2, * k3, sl 3; rep from *, end k3, sl 2, k1.
Row 6—With A, k1, sl 2, * p3, sl 3; rep from *, end p3, sl 2, k1.
Row 7—With B, k4, * sl 1, k5; rep from *, end sl 1, k4.
Row 8—With B, k1, p3, * sl 1, p5; rep from *, end sl 1, p3, k1.

Repeat Rows 1–8.

Semi-Woven Tweed

Semi-Woven Tweed

Odd number of sts. Colors A and B.

Cast on with Color A and purl one row.

Row 1 (Right side)—With B, k1, * sl 1 wyib, k1; rep from *.
Row 2—With B, purl.
Row 3—With A, k1, * sl 1 wyif, k1; rep from *.
Row 4—With A, purl.
Row 5—With B, k2, * sl 1 wyib, k1; rep from *, end k1.
Row 6—With B, purl.
Row 7—With A, k2, * sl 1 wyif, k1; rep from *, end k1.
Row 8—With A, purl.

Repeat Rows 1–8.

Woven Stripe Pattern

Here is a gay and easy-to-work pattern. It is delightful for children's garments or for ski sweaters where a colorful and informal look is desired. For a four-color version, simply work the pattern once through in colors A and B, then the second time through in colors C and D.

Odd number of sts. Colors A and B.

Row 1 (Right side)—With A, knit.
Row 2—With A, purl.
Row 3—With B, k1, * sl 1 wyif, k1; rep from *.
Row 4—With B, purl.
Row 5—With A, k2, * sl 1 wyif, k1; rep from *, end k1.
Row 6—With A, purl.
Row 7—With A, knit.
Row 8—With A, purl.
Row 9—With B, k1, * sl 1 wyif, k1; rep from *.
Row 10—With B, purl.
Rows 11 and 12—With B, repeat Rows 1 and 2.
Rows 13 and 14—With A, repeat Rows 3 and 4.
Rows 15 and 16—With B, repeat Rows 5 and 6.
Rows 17 and 18—With B, repeat Rows 7 and 8.
Rows 19 and 20—With A, repeat Rows 9 and 10.

Repeat Rows 1–20.

Woven Stripe Pattern

Three-Color Tweed

Odd number of sts. Colors A, B, and C.

Cast on with Color C.

Row 1 (Right side)—With B, k1, * sl 1 wyif, k1; rep from *.
Row 2—With B, purl.
Row 3—With A, k1, * sl 1 wyib, k1; rep from *.
Row 4—With A, purl.
Row 5—With C, k1, * sl 1 wyif, k1; rep from *.
Row 6—With C, purl.
Rows 7 and 8—With B, repeat Rows 3 and 4.
Rows 9 and 10—With A, repeat Rows 1 and 2.
Rows 11 and 12—With C, repeat Rows 3 and 4.

Repeat Rows 1–12.

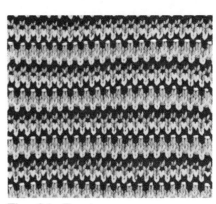

Three-Color Tweed

Bricks

This version of the checkered pattern is fun to use. It consists of knit-stitch "bricks" in one color set off by garter-stitch "mortar" in the second color.

Multiple of 4 sts plus 3. Colors A and B.

Rows 1 and 2—With A, knit. (This is the "mortar" color).
Row 3—With B, k1, * sl 1 wyib, k3; rep from * to last 2 sts, sl 1, k1. (Right side).
Row 4—With B, p1, * sl 1 wyif, p3; rep from * to last 2 sts, sl 1, p1.
Rows 5 and 6—With A, knit.
Row 7—With B, k3, * sl 1 wyib, k3; rep from *.
Row 8—With B, p3, * sl 1 wyif, p3; rep from *.

Repeat Rows 1–8.

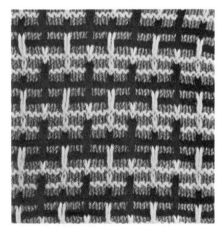

Bricks

Broken Plaid Pattern

Multiple of 8 sts plus 7.

Colors A, B, and C. Color B is the background color.

Row 1 (Right side)—With A, knit.
Row 2—With A, k3, insert needle knitwise into next st and wrap yarn 3 times around point of needle, then knit the st (k1-3 wraps); * k7, k1-3 wraps; rep from *, end k3.
Row 3—With B, k3, * sl 1 wyib, k3; rep from *. (Throughout pattern, the extra wraps are dropped from the elongated stitches when these stitches are slipped.)
Row 4—With B, p3, * sl 1 wyif, p3; rep from *.
Row 5—With C, k3, * sl 1 wyib, k7; rep from *, end sl 1, k3.
Row 6—With C, k3, * sl 1 wyif, k7; rep from *, end sl 1, k3.
Rows 7 and 8—With B, repeat Rows 3 and 4.
Row 9—With C, knit.
Row 10—With C, k7, * k1-3 wraps, k7; rep from *.
Rows 11 and 12—With B, repeat Rows 3 and 4.
Row 13—With A, k7, * sl 1 wyib, k7; rep from *.
Row 14—With A, k7, * sl 1 wyif, k7; rep from *.
Rows 15 and 16—With B, repeat Rows 3 and 4.

Repeat Rows 1–16.

Broken Plaid Pattern

Basket Stitch

Not to be confused with Basketweave or Basket Cable, the Basket Stitch works equally well in a single-color version but is most adaptable to color contrast. It may also be worked in the same manner as the Bricks pattern, i.e., with two rows of stockinette in place of four rows of garter stitch for Color B, and two rows of garter stitch for Color A in place of stockinette.

Basket Stitch

Multiple of 4 sts plus 3. Colors A and B.

Cast on with Color A and purl one row (This is the wrong side).

Rows 1 and 3—With B, k3, * sl 1 wyib, k3; rep from *.
Rows 2 and 4—With B, k3, * sl 1 wyif, k3; rep from *.
Row 5—With A, knit.
Row 6—With A, purl.

Repeat Rows 1–6.

Fancy Basket Pattern

Multiple of 4 sts plus 1. Colors A and B.

Row 1 (Wrong side)—With A, purl.
Row 2—With A, knit.
Row 3—With A, p4, * p1 wrapping yarn twice around needle, p3; rep from *, end p1.
Row 4—With B, k4, * sl 1 wyib dropping extra wrap, k3; rep from *, end k1.
Rows 5 and 7—With B, k4, * sl 1 wyif, k3; rep from *, end k1.
Row 6—With B, k4, * sl 1 wyib, k3; rep from *, end k1.
Row 8—With A, k4, * drop sl-st off needle to front of work, k2, pick up dropped st and knit it, k1; rep from *, end k1.
Rows 9, 10, and 11—With A, repeat Rows 1, 2, and 3.
Rows 12, 13, 14, and 15—With B, repeat Rows 4, 5, 6, and 7.
Row 16—With A, k2, * sl 2 wyib, drop sl-st off needle to front of work, sl the same 2 sts back to left-hand needle, pick up dropped st and knit it, k3; rep from *, end k3.

Repeat Rows 1–16.

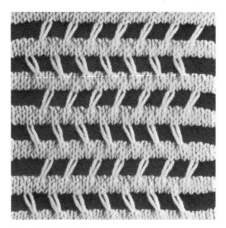
Fancy Basket Pattern

Belted Stripes

Belted Stripes

This is a simple pattern based on Basket Stitch. The pattern is elongated laterally, so that it gives the illusion of belts of contrasting color woven through a knitted fabric just as ribbons are sometimes woven through a series of eyelets. This pattern can be used very effectively in isolated areas of a garment as trimming, such as near the edges of collars, cuffs, and hem.

Multiple of 12 sts plus 9. Colors A and B.

Rows 1, 3, and 5 (Right side)—With A, knit.

Rows 2 and 4—With A, purl.

Row 6—With A, p3, * p next 3 sts wrapping yarn twice around needle for each st, p9; rep from *, end last repeat p3.

Row 7—With B, k3, * sl 3 wyib dropping extra wraps, k9; rep from *, end last repeat k3.

Rows 8 and 10—With B, k3, * sl 3 wyif, k9; rep from *, end last repeat k3.

Row 9—With B, k3, * sl 3 wyib, k9; rep from *, end last repeat k3.

Rows 11, 13, and 15—With A, knit.

Rows 12 and 14—With A, purl.

Row 16—With A, p9, * p3 wrapping yarn twice for each st, p9; rep from *.

Row 17—With B, k9, * sl 3 wyib dropping extra wraps, k9; rep from *.

Row 18—With B, k9, * sl 3 wyif, k9; rep from *.

Row 19—With B, k9, * sl 3 wyib, k9; rep from *.

Row 20—Repeat Row 18.

Repeat Rows 1–20.

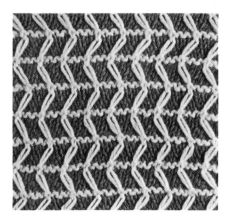

Zigzag Checks

Zigzag Checks

This pattern has another point of interest, beside that of color. The background stitches are drawn into attractive waves behind the slipped stitches of contrasting color, which lends an added dimension to the pattern.

Multiple of 4 sts.

Colors A and B. Color B is the background color. Cast on with A.

NOTE: On wrong side (odd-numbered rows) sl all sl-sts with yarn in front; on right side (even-numbered rows) sl all sl-sts with yarn in back.

Row 1 (Wrong side)—With A, * insert needle into first st knit-wise and wrap yarn twice around point of needle, then knit the st (k1-2 wraps); k3; rep from *.
Row 2—With B, * k3, sl 1 dropping extra wrap; rep from *.
Rows 3 and 5—With B, * sl 1, p3; rep from *.
Row 4—With B, * k3, sl 1; rep from *.
Row 6—With A, * sl 3 sts to right-hand needle, drop next (Color A) st off left-hand needle and leave at front, sl same 3 sts back to left-hand needle, pick up dropped st and knit it; k3; rep from *.
Row 7—With A, * k3, k1-2 wraps; rep from *.
Row 8—With B, * sl 1 dropping extra wrap, k3; rep from *.
Rows 9 and 11—With B, * p3, sl 1; rep from *.
Row 10—With B, * sl 1, k3; rep from *.
Row 12—With A, * drop first (Color A) st off needle and leave at front, k3, then pick up dropped st and knit it; rep from *.

Repeat Rows 1–12.

Staircase Pattern

Because of its strong diagonal line, this pattern is interesting in round knitting, such as for socks or seamless sweaters done on circular needles—the diagonal pattern thus becoming a spiral, the two edge sts omitted.

Multiple of 6 sts plus 2. Colors A and B.

Cast on with Color A.

Row 1 (Right side)—With B, k1, * sl 2 wyib, k4; rep from *, end k1.
Row 2—With B, k1, * p4, sl 2 wyif; rep from *, end k1.
Row 3—With A, k1, * k4, sl 2 wyib; rep from *, end k1.
Row 4—With A, k1, * sl 2 wyif, p4; rep from *, end k1.
Row 5—With B, k3, * sl 2 wyib, k4; rep from *, end sl 2, k3.
Row 6—With B, k1, p2, * sl 2 wyif, p4; rep from *, end sl 2, p2, k1.
Rows 7 and 8—With A, repeat Rows 1 and 2.
Rows 9 and 10—With B, repeat Rows 3 and 4.
Rows 11 and 12—With A, repeat Rows 5 and 6.

Repeat Rows 1–12.

Staircase Pattern

Chain Stripes

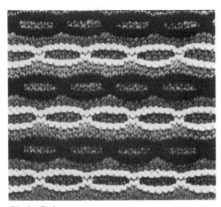

Chain Stripes

Multiple of 8 sts plus 6.

Colors A, B, and C. Color A is the background color.

Row 1 (Right side)—With A, knit.
Row 2—With A, purl.
Rows 3 and 4—With B, knit.
Row 5—With A, k6, * sl 2 wyib, k6; rep from *.
Row 6—With A, p6, * sl 2 wyif, p6; rep from *.
Row 7—With B, repeat Row 5.
Row 8—With B, knit.
Rows 9 and 10—With A, repeat Rows 1 and 2.
Rows 11 and 12—With C, knit.
Row 13—With A, k2, * sl 2 wyib, k6; rep from *, end sl 2, k2.
Row 14—With A, p2, * sl 2 wyif, p6; rep from *, end sl 2, p2.
Row 15—With C, repeat Row 13.
Row 16—With C, knit.

Repeat Rows 1–16.

Bubble Tweed

Bubble Tweed

Here is an interesting tweed with a subtle diagonal line. The pattern moves one stitch to the right every other row.

NOTE: On right-side rows sl all sl-sts with yarn in back. On wrong-side rows sl all sl-sts with yarn in front.

Multiple of 3 sts plus 2. Colors A and B.

Cast on with Color B and purl one row.

Row 1 (Right side)—With A, k1, * sl 1, ssk, lift running thread between st just worked and next st, and knit in back loop of this thread (Make One or M1); rep from *, end k1.
Row 2—With A, p1, * p2, sl 1; rep from *, end p1.
Row 3—With B, k2, * sl 1, ssk, M1; rep from *, end sl 1, k2.
Row 4—With B, p2, * sl 1, p2; rep from *.
Row 5—With A, k3, * sl 1, ssk, M1; rep from *, end sl 1, k1.
Row 6—With A, p1, * sl 1, p2; rep from *, end p1.
Rows 7 and 8—With B, repeat Rows 1 and 2.
Rows 9 and 10—With A, repeat Rows 3 and 4.
Rows 11 and 12—With B, repeat Rows 5 and 6.

Repeat Rows 1–12.

Star Tweed

A soft, thick tweed pattern that can make beautiful and unusual coats and suits. The technique is a little different from most slip-stitch color patterns, but it is quickly mastered and works smoothly and rapidly.

Multiple of 4 sts plus 1. Colors A and B.

Cast on with B and purl one row.

Row 1 (Right side)—With A, k1, * sl 1 wyib, insert needle under running thread between the st just slipped and the next st, and knit this thread; sl 1 wyib, k1, then pass first slipped st over 3 sts; k1; rep from *.

Row 2—With A, purl.

Row 3—With B, k3, * rep from * of Row 1, end k2.

Row 4—With B, purl.

Repeat Rows 1–4.

Star Tweed

Hexagon Pattern

This is a variation of the Checkered Pattern, in which the slipped stitches pull the garter stitch rows out of line upward and downward, to form hexagons. If desired, a third color can be introduced in Rows 13 through 18.

Multiple of 8 sts plus 6. Colors A and B.

Rows 1 and 2—With A, knit. (Odd-numbered rows are right-side rows.)

Rows 3, 5, and 7—With B, k2, * sl 2 wyib, k6; rep from *, end sl 2, k2.

Rows 4, 6, and 8—With B, p2, * sl 2 wyif, p6; rep from *, end sl 2, p2.

(Throughout these six rows the same A sts are slipped.)

Rows 9, 10, 11, and 12—With A, knit.

Rows 13, 15, and 17—With B, k6, * sl 2 wyib, k6; rep from *.

Rows 14, 16, and 18—With B, p6, * sl 2 wyif, p6; rep from *.

Rows 19 and 20—With A, knit.

Repeat Rows 1–20.

Hexagon Pattern

Clouds and Mountains

Clouds and Mountains

Intriguingly textured, this pattern works on the same principle as the Hexagon Pattern—that is, by straining the slip-stitches upward over 8 rows so that they distort the rows they span. The result is a "different" kind of check arranged roughly in triangles.

Multiple of 8 sts plus 6. Colors A and B.

Cast on with A and purl one row.

Row 1 (Right side)—With B, knit.
Row 2—With B, k6, * sl 2 wyif, k6; rep from *.
Row 3—With B, k6, * sl 2 wyib, k6; rep from *.
Row 4—With B, repeat Row 2.
Rows 5 and 7—With A, k6, * sl 2 wyib, k6; rep from *.
Rows 6 and 8—With A, p6, * sl 2 wyif, p6; rep from *.
Row 9—With B, knit.
Row 10—With B, k2, * sl 2 wyif, k6; rep from *, end sl 2, k2.
Row 11—With B, k2, * sl 2 wyib, k6; rep from *, end sl 2, k2.
Row 12—With B, repeat Row 10.
Rows 13 and 15—With A, k2, * sl 2 wyib, k6; rep from *, end sl 2, k2.
Rows 14 and 16—With A, p2, * sl 2 wyif, p6; rep from *, end sl 2, p2.

Repeat Rows 1–16.

Tweed Knot Stitch

Tweed Knot Stitch

In blocking, this pattern should not be too much stretched, so that the purled "knots" can remain close together for a nubby effect.

Odd number of sts. Colors A and B.

Row 1 (Wrong side)—With A, knit.
Row 2—With A, k1, * k next st in the row below, k1; rep from *.
Row 3—With B, knit.
Row 4—With B, k2, * k next st in the row below, k1; rep from *, end k1.

Repeat Rows 1–4.

Blister Check, or Coin Stitch

In this pattern the drop-stitch technique is used to make a very attractive fabric with the double interest of color and texture.

Multiple of 4 sts plus 1.

Colors A and B. Cast on with A and knit one row.

Row 1 (Wrong side)—With A, purl.
Rows 2 and 4—With B, knit.
Rows 3 and 5—With B, purl.
Row 6—With A, k2, * drop next st off needle and unravel 4 rows down, picking up the Color A st from Row 1 below; insert needle into this st and under the 4 loose strands of Color B, and knit, catching the 4 loose strands behind st; k3; rep from *, end last repeat k2.
Row 7—With A, purl.
Rows 8 and 10—With B, knit.
Rows 9 and 11—With B, purl.
Row 12—With A, k4, * drop next st, unravel, and knit Color A st from 5th row below as in Row 6; k3; rep from *, end k1.

Repeat Rows 1–12.

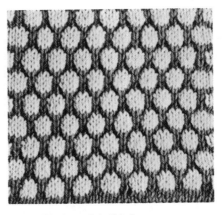

Blister Check, or Coin Stitch

Zebra Chevron

NOTE: On all right-side rows (odd numbers) all sl-sts are slipped with yarn in back. On wrong-side rows (even numbers) all sl-sts are slipped with yarn in front.

Multiple of 24 sts plus 2. Colors A and B.

Cast on with Color A and purl one row.

Row 1 (Right side)—With B, k1, * sl 1, k2; rep from *, end k1.
Row 2—With B, k1, * p2, sl 1; rep from *, end k1.
Row 3—With A, k1, * k1, sl 1, (k2, sl 1) 3 times, k3, (sl 1, k2) 3 times, sl 1; rep from *, end k1.
Row 4—With A, k1, * sl 1, (p2, sl 1) 3 times, p3, (sl 1, p2) 3 times, sl 1, p1; rep from *, end k1.
Row 5—With B, k1, * k2, (sl 1, k2) 3 times, sl 1, k1, sl 1, (k2, sl 1) 3 times, k1; rep from *, end k1.
Row 6—With B, k1, * p1, (sl 1, p2) 3 times, sl 1, pl, sl 1, (p2, sl 1) 3 times, p2; rep from *, end k1.
Rows 7 and 8—With A, repeat Rows 1 and 2.
Rows 9 and 10—With B, repeat Rows 3 and 4.
Rows 11 and 12—With A, repeat Rows 5 and 6.

Repeat Rows 1–12.

Zebra Chevron

Two-Color Cable Rib

Two-Color Cable Rib

This is the Slipped Cable Rib pattern, which looks very effective in two colors.

Multiple of 8 sts plus 2. Colors A and B.

Row 1 (Wrong side)—With A, k2, * p6, k2; rep from *.
Row 2—With A, p2, * sl 1 wyib, k4, sl 1 wyib, p2; rep from *.
Row 3—With B, k2, * sl 1 wyif, p4, sl 1 wyif, k2; rep from *.
Rows 4 and 5—With B, repeat Rows 2 and 3.
Row 6—With B, p2, * drop sl-st off needle to front of work, k2, then pick up sl-st and knit it (taking care that sl-st is not twisted); sl next 2 sts to right-hand needle, drop next sl-st off needle to front of work, then sl the 2 sts back to left-hand needle, pick up dropped st with right needle, replace it on left needle and knit it; k2, p2; rep from *.

Repeat Rows 1–6.

Yarn-Over Check

Yarn-Over Check

The technique of making this pattern is interesting and novel. Because of the use of yarn-over stitches, the fabric tends to be loose and fluffy, with a good deal of lateral spread. Care must be taken not to cast on too many stitches.

Odd number of sts. Colors A and B.

Cast on with Color A and knit one row.

Row 1 (Right side)—With B, p1, * yo, sl 1 wyib, p1; rep from *. (The yo is taken over the top of the needle and held in back of the slipped st, then brought forward again for the next p st.)
Row 2—With B, k1, * yo, sl the sl-st and the yo of previous row together wyib, k1; rep from *.
Row 3—With A, p1, * k3 tog (the sl-st and the two yo sts), p1; rep from *.
Row 4—With A, k1, * yo, sl 1 wyib, k1; rep from *.
Row 5—With A, p1, * yo, sl the sl-st and the yo of previous row wyib, p1; rep from *.
Row 6—With A, k1, * p3 tog (the sl-st and the two yo sts), k1; rep from *.

Repeat Rows 1–6.

Shadow Box Pattern

Although it is one of the simplest of three-color patterns, the Shadow Box is very striking. It uses color, rather than texture, to give the impression of a heavily sculptured surface.

Multiple of 4 sts plus 3.

Colors A, B, and C.

Row 1 (Right side)—With A, knit.
Row 2—With A, k1, * k1 wrapping yarn twice around needle, k3; rep from *, end last repeat k1.
Row 3—With B, k1, * sl 1 wyib dropping extra wrap, k3; rep from *, end last repeat k1.
Row 4—With B, k1, * sl 1 wyif, k3; rep from *, end sl 1, k1.
Row 5—With C, k1, * sl 2 wyib, k2; rep from *, end sl 1, k1.
Row 6—With C, k1, sl 1 wyif, * p2, sl 2 wyif; rep from *, end k1.

Repeat Rows 1–6.

Shadow Box Pattern

Beaded Stripe Pattern

This pattern is excellent for sweaters, and is very effective when worked in fine yarn. Like many of the tweed-type patterns, it is interesting as a sort of optical illusion: it can be seen as dark strings of "beads" on a light background, or as light ones on a dark background.

Multiple of 6 sts plus 5. Colors A and B.

Row 1 (Right side)—With A, knit.
Row 2—With A, k1, * p3, k3; rep from *, end p3, k1.
Row 3—With B, k1, * sl 3 wyib, k3; rep from *, end sl 3, k1.
Row 4—With B, k1, p1, * sl 1 wyif, p5; rep from *, end sl 1, p1, k1.
Row 5—With B, knit.
Row 6—With B, k4, * p3, k3; rep from *, end k1.
Row 7—With A, k4, * sl 3 wyib, k3; rep from *, end k1.
Row 8—With A, k1, p4, * sl 1 wyif, p5; rep from *, end sl 1, p4, k1.

Repeat Rows 1–8.

Beaded Stripe Pattern

Striped Quilting Pattern

Striped Quilting Pattern

This delightful pattern makes a honeycomb-like lattice of diamond shapes against a background of striped Garter Stitch. The fabric is dense both vertically and horizontally.

Multiple of 6 sts plus 2. Colors A and B.

Row 1 (Wrong side)—With A, k1, * p1, k4, p1; rep from *, end k1.

Row 2—With B, k1, * sl 1 wyib, k4, sl 1 wyib; rep from *, end k1.

Row 3—With B, k1, * sl 1 wyif, k4, sl 1 wyif; rep from *, end k1.

Row 4—With A, k1, * drop Color A sl-st to front of work, k2, pick up dropped st and knit it; sl 2 wyib, drop Color A sl-st to front of work, sl the same 2 sts back to left-hand needle, pick up dropped st and knit it, k2; rep from *, end k1.

Row 5—With A, k1, * k2, p2, k2; rep from *, end k1.

Row 6—With B, k1, * k2, sl 2 wyib, k2; rep from *, end k1.

Row 7—With B, k1, * k2, sl 2 wyif, k2; rep from *, end k1.

Row 8—With A, k1, * sl 2 wyib, drop Color A sl-st to front of work, sl the same 2 sts back to left-hand needle, pick up dropped st and knit it, k2, drop Color A sl-st to front of work, k2, pick up dropped st and knit it; rep from *, end k1.

Repeat Rows 1–8.

Royal Quilting

Royal Quilting

Royally beautiful, indeed, is this two-color quilting pattern which can hardly be surpassed for novelty and ingenuity. The fabric is firm, close, and somewhat restrained from excessive curling by the strands of Color A which are carried across the *wrong* side on Rows 4 and 8. On these rows, as well as on Rows 1 and 5 (when the strands are carried on the *right* side), be sure to keep a *very* light tension on the strands so that they do not "squeeze" the pattern.

Royal Quilting is a wonderful pattern for cushion covers, hats, slippers, and garment accents such as collars, cuffs, and pockets, as well as making delightful sweaters and jackets when used all over the garment.

Multiple of 6 sts plus 3. Colors A and B.

Row 1 (Wrong side)—With A, k1, p1, * sl 5 wyib, p1; rep from *, end k1.

Row 2—With B, knit.

Row 3—With B, k1, purl to last st, k1.

Row 4—With A, k1, sl 3 wyib, * insert needle under the loose strand of Row 1 and knit the next st bringing st out under strand to catch strand behind st; sl 5 wyib; rep from * to last 5 sts, end knit next st under loose strand, sl 3 wyib, k1.

Row 5—With A, k1, sl 3 wyib, * p1, sl 5 wyib; rep from * to last 5 sts, end p1, sl 3 wyib, k1.

Rows 6 and 7—With B, repeat Rows 2 and 3.

Row 8—With A, k1, * knit next st under loose strand of Row 5, sl 5 wyib; rep from * to last 2 sts, end knit next st under loose strand, k1.

Repeat Rows 1–8.

Criss Cross Pattern

For a test swatch, cast on a minimum of 22 sts.

Multiple of 10 sts plus 2. Colors A and B.

Cast on with Color A and knit one row.

Row 1 (Wrong side)—With A, k3, * k1 wrapping yarn 3 times around needle, k4; rep from *, end last repeat k3.

Row 2—With B, k3, * sl 1 wyib dropping extra wraps, k4; rep from *, end last repeat k3.

Rows 3 and 5—With B, p3, * sl 1 wyif, p4; rep from *, end last repeat p3.

Row 4—With B, k3, * sl 1 wyib, k4; rep from *, end last repeat k3.

Row 6—With A, k3, * drop 1st Color A sl-st off needle to front of work, sl next 4 sts wyib, drop 2nd Color A sl-st off needle to front of work, sl the same 4 sts back to left-hand needle, pick up *2nd* dropped st and knit it, k4 (these are the same 4 Color B sts that were slipped before), then pick up the *1st* dropped st and knit it, k4; rep from *, end last repeat k3.

Rows 7 through 11—Repeat Rows 1 through 5.

Row 12—With A, k1, sl 2 wyib, drop Color A sl-st off needle to front of work, sl the same 2 sts back to left-hand needle, pick up dropped st and knit it, k6, *, rep from * of Row 6 across to last 4 sts, end: drop Color A sl-st off needle to front of work, k2, pick up dropped st and knit it, k1.

Repeat Rows 1–12.

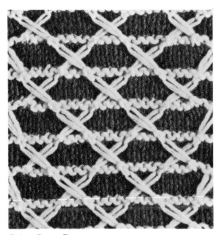

Criss Cross Pattern

Fancy Bricks *See color page viii*

This charming three-color version of "Bricks" is done with elongated slip-stitches. Since the slipped stitches must be carried up for six rows, they are loosened by making extra turns around the needle at the base of the stitch. When thus elongated, the slipped stitches will not deform the horizontal rows to which they are attached.

Multiple of 4 sts plus 3.

Colors A, B, and C; Color B is the background color.

Row 1 (Right side)—With A, knit.
Row 2—With A, k3, * insert needle into next st as if to knit, then wrap yarn 3 times around point of needle, then knit the st carrying extra loops on needle; k3; rep from *.
Row 3—With B, k3, * sl 1 wyib dropping extra wraps off needle, k3; rep from *.
Row 4—With B, p3, * sl 1 wyif, p3; rep from *.
Row 5—With C, k3, * sl 1 wyib, k3; rep from *.
Row 6—With C, k3, * sl 1 wyif, k3; rep from *.
Row 7—With B, k3, * sl 1 wyib, k3; rep from *.
Row 8—With B, repeat Row 4.
Row 9—With A, knit.
Row 10—With A, k1, * k1 wrapping yarn 3 times as in row 2, k3; rep from *, end last rep k1.
Row 11—With B, k1, * sl 1 wyib dropping extra wraps, k3; rep from *, end last rep k1.
Row 12—With B, p1, * sl 1 wyif, p3; rep from *, end last rep p1.
Row 13—With C, k1, * sl 1 wyib, k3; rep from *, end last rep k1.
Row 14—With C, k1, * sl 1 wyif, k3; rep from *, end last rep k1.
Row 15—With B, k1, * sl 1 wyib, k3; rep from *, end last rep k1.
Row 16—With B, repeat Row 12.

Repeat Rows 1–16.

Tricolor Basket Plaid *See color page ix*

A delightful three-color plaid pattern that looks more complicated than it really is. In this pattern, as in "Fancy Bricks", the slip-stitches are elongated to span six rows. There are four preparatory rows which are omitted from subsequent repeats. To bind off, knit one row plain and then bind off; or finish with four final rows as illustrated.

Multiple of 8 sts plus 7.

Colors A, B, and C; Color B is the background color.

Row 1 (Right side)—With A, knit.

Row 2—With A, k3, insert needle into next st as if to knit and wrap yarn 3 times around point of needle, then knit the st carrying extra loops on needle; this is called k1-3 wraps; * k7, k1-3 wraps; rep from *, end k3.

Row 3—With B, k3, sl 1 wyib dropping extra wraps off needle, * k7, sl 1 wyib dropping extra wraps; rep from *, end k3.

Row 4—With B, p3, sl 1 wyif, * p7, sl 1 wyif; rep from *, end p3.

End of preparation rows.

Row 5—With C, k3, sl 1 wyib, * k7, sl 1 wyib; rep from *, end k3.

Row 6—With C, * k3, sl 1 wyif, k3, k1-3 wraps; rep from *, end k3, sl 1 wyif, k3.

Row 7—With B, * k3, sl 1 wyib, k3, sl 1 wyib dropping extra wraps; rep from *, end k3, sl 1 wyib, k3.

Row 8—With B, p3, * sl 1 wyif, p3; rep from *.

Row 9—With A, k7, * sl 1 wyib, k7; rep from *.

Row 10—With A, * k3, k1-3 wraps, k3, sl 1 wyif; rep from *, end k3, k1-3 wraps, k3.

Row 11—With B, * k3, sl 1 wyib dropping extra wraps, k3, sl 1 wyib; rep from *, end k3, sl 1 wyib dropping extra wraps, k3.

Row 12—With B, p3, * sl 1 wyif, p3; rep from *.

Repeat Rows 5-12.

Navajo Basket *See color page ix*

This is a pleasing combination of variation Basket Stitch and a two-color Woven Stitch.

Multiple of 4 sts plus 3. Colors A, B, and C.

Row 1 (Right side)—With A, knit.

Row 2—With A, purl.

Row 3—With B, k1, * sl 1 wyif, k1; rep from *.

Row 4—With B, purl.

Row 5—With A, k2, * sl 1 wyif, k1; rep from *, end k1.

Row 6—With A, purl.

Rows 7 and 9—With C, k1, * sl 1 wyib, k3; rep from *, end last rep k1.

Rows 8 and 10—With C, p1, * sl 1 wyif, p3; rep from *, end last rep p1.

Repeat Rows 1-10.

Three-Color Basket Tweed

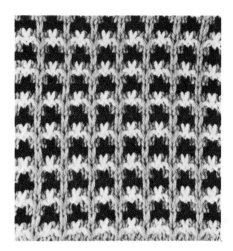

Three-Color Basket Tweed

This is a simple and easy pattern with a remarkably striking effect. For possible variations, try reversing the knits and purls (i.e., purl in Rows 2 and 6, knit in Rows 4 and 8) or working the entire pattern in garter stitch fashion (i.e., knit wrong-side rows) as in Three-and-One Tweed.

Multiple of 4 sts plus 1.

Colors A, B, and C. Cast on with Color A and purl one row.

Row 1 (Right side)—With B, k1, * k3, sl 1 wyib; rep from *, and k4.
Row 2—With B, k1, * k3, sl 1 wyif; rep from *, end k4.
Row 3—With A, k2, * sl 1 wyib, k3; rep from *, end sl 1, k2.
Row 4—With A, p2, * sl 1 wyif, p3; rep from *, end sl 1, p2.
Rows 5 and 6—With C, repeat Rows 1 and 2.
Rows 7 and 8—With A, repeat Rows 3 and 4.

Repeat Rows 1–8.

Motley Check

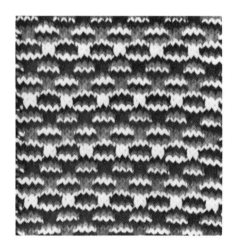

Motley Check

The constant alternation of three different strands of color gives this a most unusual appearance. Worked in three strongly contrasting, bright colors, it is gay and brilliant; worked in three colors that are close together in hue or tone, it is a subtle mixture.

Multiple of 6 sts plus 4. Colors A, B, and C.

Cast on with Color C.

Row 1 (Right side)—With A, knit.
Row 2—With B, purl.
Row 3—With C, k1, * sl 2 wyib, k4; rep from *, end sl 2, k1.
Row 4—With A, p1, * sl 2 wyif, p4; rep from *, end sl 2, p1.
Row 5—With B, knit.
Row 6—With C, purl.
Row 7—With A, k4, * sl 2 wyib, k4; rep from *.
Row 8—With B, p4, * sl 2 wyif, p4; rep from *.
Rows 9–24—Repeat Rows 1–8 twice more, changing colors every row.

Repeat Rows 1–24.

Three-and-One Check

This is a pretty variation on the "Bricks" theme. With the addition of extra rows, the bricks take on a rather arched shape.

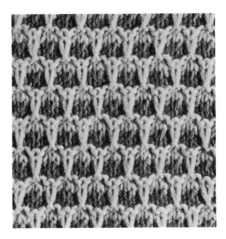

Multiple of 4 sts plus 3. Colors A and B.

Row 1 (Right side)—With A, knit.
Row 2—With A, knit.
Row 3—With B, k1, * sl 1 wyib, k3; rep from *, end sl 1, k1.
Row 4—With B, p1, * sl 1 wyif, p3; rep from *, end sl 1, p1.
Row 5—With A, k1, * sl 1 wyib, k1; rep from *.
Row 6—With A, p1, * sl 1 wyif, p3; rep from *, end sl 1, p1.
Rows 7 and 8—With A, knit.
Row 9—With B, k3, * sl 1 wyib, k3; rep from *.
Row 10—With B, p3, * sl 1 wyif, p3; rep from *.
Row 11—With A, k1, * sl 1 wyib, k1; rep from *.
Row 12—With A, p3, * sl 1 wyif, p3; rep from *.

Repeat Rows 1–12.

Three-and-One Check

Rippled Chevron

This pattern is similar to Zebra Chevron but it is wider, and has a faintly Oriental flavor. Patterns like this can be found in Persian rugs, Turkish mosaic work and the like.

Multiple of 16 sts plus 3. Colors A and B.

Cast on with Color A and purl one row.

Row 1 (Right side)—With B, k1, sl 1 wyib, * k3, sl 1 wyib; rep from *, end k1.
Row 2—With B, k1, sl 1 wyif, * p3, sl 1 wyif; rep from *, end k1.
Row 3—With A, k4, * sl 1 wyib, k3, sl 1 wyib, k1, sl 1 wyib, k3, sl 1 wyib, k5; rep from *, end last repeat k4.
Row 4—With A, k1, p3, * sl 1 wyif, p3, sl 1 wyif, p1, sl 1 wyif, p3, sl 1 wyif, p5; rep from *, end last repeat p3, k1.
Row 5—With B, k3, * sl 1 wyib, k3; rep from *.
Row 6—With B, k1, p2, * sl 1 wyif, p3; rep from *, end sl 1 wyif, p2, k1.
Row 7—With A, k2, * sl 1 wyib, k3, sl 1 wyib, k5, sl 1 wyib, k3, sl 1 wyib, k1; rep from *, end k1.
Row 8—With A, k1, p1, * sl 1 wyif, p3, sl 1 wyif, p5, sl 1 wyif, p3, sl 1 wyif, p1; rep from *, end k1.

Repeat Rows 1–8.

Rippled Chevron

Gull Check

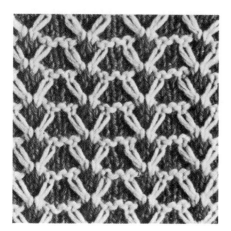

Gull Check

Here is a beautiful pattern in which a cable can be traced, translated into two colors and repeated continuously across the fabric. It is a good example of a classic pattern subjected to a novel treatment.

Multiple of 7 sts plus 1. Colors A and B.

Row 1 (Wrong side)—With A, k3, * p2, k5; rep from *, end p2, k3.

Rows 2 and 4—With B, k3, * sl 2 wyib, k5; rep from *, end sl 2, k3.

Rows 3 and 5—With B, p3, * sl 2 wyif, p5; rep from *, end sl 2, p3.

Row 6—With A, * k1, sl 2 wyib, drop Color A sl-st off needle to front of work, sl the same 2 sts back to left-hand needle, pick up dropped st and knit it; k2, drop next Color A sl-st off needle to front of work, k2, pick up dropped st and knit it; rep from *, end k1.

Repeat Rows 1–6.

Triple Torch

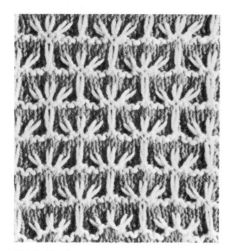

Triple Torch

The directions for this pattern seem complicated, but it is actually simple to work. The knitter can easily grasp the pattern principle in the first 16 rows and thereafter work by looking only at the fabric.

A variation can be made by repeating Rows 1–8 only. This produces a kind of Basket Stitch with wide blocks, the small triple flare being reproduced in each block, one above the other. The last eight rows out of the sixteen only serve to alternate the patterns.

Multiple of 10 sts plus 3. Colors A and B.

Row 1 (Right side)—With A, knit.

Row 2—With A, k1, k1 wrapping yarn twice around needle, * k3, k3 wrapping yarn twice for each st, k3, k1 wrapping yarn twice; rep from *, end k1.

Row 3—With B, k1, sl 1 wyib, * k3, sl 3 wyib, k3, sl 1 wyib; rep from *, end k1. (On this row drop all extra wraps as the wrapped sts are slipped.)

Rows 4 and 6—With B, p1, sl 1 wyif, * p3, sl 3 wyif, p3, sl 1 wyif; rep from *, end p1.

Row 5—With B, repeat Row 3.

Row 7—With B, k1, sl 1 wyib, * k1, sl 2 wyib, drop the *first* st of the group of 3 sl-sts off needle to front of work, sl the same 2 sts back to left-hand needle, pick up dropped st and knit it, k2, sl 1 wyib (this is the 2nd sl-st of the group), drop next (3rd) sl-st off needle to front of work, k2, pick up dropped st and knit it, k1, sl 1 wyib; rep from *, end k1.

Row 8—With B, p1, * sl 1 wyif, p9; rep from *, end sl 1, p1.

Row 9—With A, knit.

Row 10—With A, k1, k2 wrapping yarn twice for each st, * k3, k1 wrapping yarn twice, k3, k3 wrapping yarn twice for each st; rep from *, end last repeat k2 wrapping yarn twice for each st, k1.

Row 11—With B, k1, sl 2 wyib, * k3, sl 1 wyib, k3, sl 3 wyib; rep from *, end last repeat sl 2 wyib, k1. (On this row all extra wraps are dropped as in Row 3.)

Rows 12 and 14—With B, p1, sl 2 wyif, * p3, sl 1 wyif, p3, sl 3 wyif; rep from *, end last repeat sl 2 wyif, p1.

Row 13—With B, repeat Row 11.

Row 15—With B, k1, * sl 1 wyib, drop next sl-st off needle to front of work, k2, pick up dropped st and knit it, k1, sl 1 wyib, k1, sl 2 wyib, drop next sl-st off needle to front of work, sl the same 2 sts back to left-hand needle, pick up dropped st and knit it, k2; rep from *, end sl 1 wyib, k1.

Row 16—With B, p6, sl 1 wyif, * p9, sl 1 wyif; rep from *, end p6.

Repeat Rows 1–16.

Linked Stripe Pattern

This is a very simple pattern that demonstrates how effective an uncomplicated two-color design can be. If Rows 9–16 are omitted, the first eight rows of the pattern will give a kind of check linking solid vertical ribs of Color A.

Multiple of 4 sts. Colors A and B.

NOTE: odd-numbered rows are right-side rows.

Rows 1, 2, 5, and 6—With A, knit.

Rows 3 and 7—With B, k1, * sl 2 wyib, k2; rep from *, end sl 2, k1.

Rows 4 and 8—With B, p1, * sl 2 wyif, p2; rep from *, end sl 2, p1.

Rows 9, 10, 13, and 14—With B, knit.

Rows 11 and 15—With A, k1, * sl 2 wyib, k2; rep from *, end sl 2, k1.

Rows 12 and 16—With A, p1, * sl 2 wyif, p2; rep from *, end sl 2, p1.

Repeat Rows 1–16.

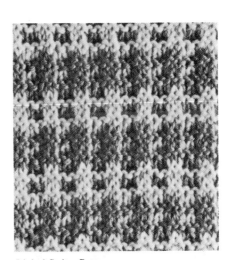

Linked Stripe Pattern

Chickenwire Check

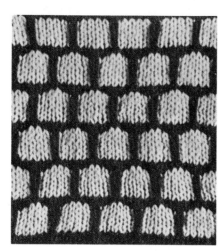

Chickenwire Check

This is a scaled-down version of the classic Hexagon Pattern that gives a somewhat lighter and looser fabric. It is quite pretty when worked in fine yarn.

Multiple of 6 sts plus 3. Colors A and B.

Row 1 (Right side)—With A, knit.

Row 2—With A, purl.

Rows 3, 5, and 7—With B, k1, * sl 1 wyib, k5; rep from *, end sl 1, k1.

Rows 4, 6, and 8—With B, p1, * sl 1 wyif, p5; rep from *, end sl 1, p1.

Rows 9 and 10—With A, repeat Rows 1 and 2.

Rows 11, 13, and 15—With B, k4, * sl 1 wyib, k5; rep from *, end sl 1, k4.

Rows 12, 14, and 16—With B, p4, * sl 1 wyif, p5; rep from *, end sl 1, p4.

Repeat Rows 1–16.

Eccentric Check

Multiple of 6 sts plus 5. Colors A and B.

Row 1 (Right side)—With A, knit.

Row 2—With A, k1, purl to last st, k1.

Row 3—With B, k1, * k4, sl 2 wyib; rep from *, end k4.

Row 4—With B, * k4, sl 2 wyif; rep from *, end k5.

Row 5—With A, k3, * sl 2 wyib, k4; rep from *, end sl 1, k1.

Row 6—With A, k1, sl 1 wyif, * p4, sl 2 wyif; rep from *, end p2, k1.

Row 7—With B, k1, * sl 2 wyib, k4; rep from *, end sl 2, k2.

Row 8—With B, k2, * sl 2 wyif, k4; rep from *, end sl 2, k1.

Rows 9 and 10—With A, repeat Rows 1 and 2.

Row 11—With B, * k4, sl 2 wyib; rep from *, end k5.

Row 12—With B, k5, * sl 2 wyif, k4; rep from *.

Row 13—With A, k1, sl 1 wyib, * k4, sl 2 wyib; rep from *, end k3.

Row 14—With A, k1, p2, * sl 2 wyif, p4; rep from *, end sl 1, k1.

Row 15—With B, k2, * sl 2 wyib, k4; rep from *, end sl 2, k1.

Row 16—With B, k1, * sl 2 wyif, k4; rep from *, end sl 2, k2.

Eccentric Check

Repeat Rows 1–16.

Elongated-Stitch Waves

Due to the loosening effect of the elongated stitches, this fabric will spread. Take the gauge carefully from a blocked test swatch, and beware of casting on too many stitches.

Elongated-Stitch Waves

Multiple of 8 sts plus 6. Colors A and B.

Row 1 (Right side)—With A, k1, * k4 wrapping yarn twice around needle for each st, k4; rep from *, end last repeat k1.

Rows 2 and 4—With A, p1, * p4 wrapping yarn twice for each st and dropping the extra wrap of previous row, p4; rep from *, end last repeat p1.

Row 3—With A, k1, * k4 wrapping yarn twice for each st and dropping the extra wrap of previous row, k4; rep from *, end last repeat k1.

Row 5—With B, knit. (All elongated sts are knitted once, and all extra wraps of previous row are dropped.)

Row 6—With B, knit.

Row 7—With A, k5, * k4 wrapping yarn twice for each st, k4; rep from *, end k1.

Rows 8 and 10—With A, p5, * p4 wrapping yarn twice for each st and dropping extra wrap of previous row, p4; rep from *, end p1.

Row 9—With A, k5, * k4 wrapping yarn twice for each st and dropping extra wrap of previous row, k4; rep from *, end k1.

Rows 11 and 12—With B, repeat Rows 5 and 6.

Repeat Rows 1–12.

Triple L Tweed

This pattern makes a thick fabric, good for coats, suits, afghans, etc. The L-shaped spots of color alternate in an interesting nubby pattern, and seem to be shadowing each other in diagonal lines.

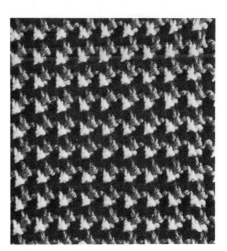

Triple L Tweed

Multiple of 3 sts plus 1. Colors A, B, and C.

Cast on with Color A and knit one row.

Row 1 (Right side)—With B, k3, * sl 1 wyib, k2; rep from *, end k1.

Row 2—With B, k3, * sl 1 wyif, k2; rep from *, end k1.

Row 3—With C, * k2, sl 1 wyib; rep from *, end k1.

Row 4—With C, k1, * sl 1 wyif, k2; rep from *.

Row 5—With A, k1, * sl 1 wyib, k2; rep from *.

Row 6—With A, * k2, sl 1 wyif; rep from *, end k1.

Repeat Rows 1–6.

Dots and Dashes

Dots and Dashes

Multiple of 10 sts plus 7. Colors A and B.

Row 1 (Right side)—With A, knit.
Row 2—With A, purl.
Row 3—With B, k1, * k5, sl 2 wyib, k1, sl 2 wyib; rep from *, end k6.
Row 4—With B, k1, * k5, sl 2 wyif, k1, sl 2 wyif; rep from *, end k6.
Rows 5 and 6—With A, repeat Rows 1 and 2.
Row 7—With B, k1, * sl 2 wyib, k1, sl 2 wyib, k5; rep from *, end last repeat k1.
Row 8—With B, k1, * sl 2 wyif, k1, sl 2 wyif, k5; rep from *, end last repeat k1.

Repeat Rows 1–8.

Fretwork Pattern

Here is a stunning slip-stitch color design based on the famous Greek Fret, a class of patterns favored by the ancients for architectural ornamentation as well as for that of clothing. Adapted to a knitting pattern, it appears intricate but the technique is a straightforward one.

Multiple of 10 sts plus 2. Colors A and B.

Note: On all right-side (odd-numbered) rows slip all sl-sts with yarn in back; on all wrong-side (even-numbered) rows slip all sl-sts with yarn in front.

Row 1 (Right side)—With A, knit.
Row 2—With A, purl.
Row 3—With B, k1, * k8, sl 2; rep from *, end k1.
Row 4 and all subsequent wrong-side rows—Using the same color as in previous row, purl across, slipping wyif all the same sts that were slipped on previous row.
Row 5—With A, k1, * sl 2, k4, sl 2, k2; rep from *, end k1.
Row 7—With B, k1, * k2, sl 2, k4, sl 2; rep from *, end k1.
Row 9—With A, k1, * sl 2, k8; rep from *, end k1.
Row 11—With B, knit.
Row 13—With A, * k4, sl 2, k4; rep from *, end k2.
Row 15—With B, k2, * sl 2, k2, sl 2, k4; rep from *.
Row 17—With A, * k4, sl 2, k2, sl 2; rep from *, end k2.
Row 19—With B, * k6, sl 2, k2; rep from *, end k2.
Row 20—See Row 4.

Repeat Rows 1–20.

Fretwork Pattern

Two Color-Reversal Patterns: Night-and-Day Stripe, and Nordic Stripe Pattern

Both of these patterns consist of horizontal stripes, each stripe bearing accents of the opposite color. Both variations are made by adding more plain knit and purl rows to the basic pattern. Further variations can be obtained by working some of the rows in Garter Stitch (knitting on the wrong side) or by purling Rows 4 and 10 in Nordic Stripe Pattern.

NIGHT-AND-DAY STRIPE

Multiple of 4 sts plus 2. Colors A and B.

Row 1 (Right side)—With A, knit.

Row 2—With A, purl.

Row 3—With B, k1, sl 1 wyib, * k2, sl 2 wyib; rep from *, end k2, sl 1, k1.

Row 4—With B, p1, sl 1 wyif, * p2, sl 2 wyif; rep from *, end p2, sl 1, p1.

Rows 5 and 6—With A, repeat Rows 1 and 2.

Rows 7 and 8—With B, repeat Rows 1 and 2.

Row 9—With A, k2, * sl 2 wyib, k2; rep from *.

Row 10—With A, p2, * sl 2 wyif, p2; rep from *.

Rows 11 and 12—With B, repeat Rows 1 and 2.

Repeat Rows 1–12.

ABOVE: *Night-and-Day Stripe*
BELOW: *Nordic Stripe Pattern*

NORDIC STRIPE PATTERN

Multiple of 4 sts plus 3. Colors A and B.

Row 1 (Right side)—With A, knit.

Row 2—With A, purl.

Row 3—With B, k1, * sl 1 wyib, k3; rep from *, end sl 1, k1.

Row 4—With B, k1, * sl 1 wyif, k3; rep from *, end sl 1, k1.

Row 5—With A, k3, * sl 1 wyib, k3; rep from *.

Row 6—With A, p3, * sl 1 wyif, p3; rep from *.

Rows 7 and 8—With A, repeat Rows 1 and 2.

Rows 9 through 16—Repeat Rows 1 through 8 reversing colors: B for 9 and 10, A for 11 and 12, B for 13, 14, 15, and 16.

Repeat Rows 1–16.

Embroidery Check Pattern

Embroidery Check Pattern

Multiple of 8 sts plus 5. Colors A and B.

Cast on with Color A and purl one row.

Row 1 (Right side)—With B, k5, * sl 3 wyib, k5; rep from *.

Row 2—With B, k2, p1, k2, * sl 3 wyif, k2, p1, k2; rep from *.

Row 3—With A, k2, * sl 1 wyib, k7; rep from *, end sl 1, k2.

Row 4—With A, k1, p1, * sl 1 wyif, p7; rep from *, end sl 1, p1, k1.

Rows 5, 6, and 7—Repeat Rows 1, 2, and 3.

Row 8—With A, k1, purl to last st, k1.

Row 9—With B, k1, * sl 3 wyib, k5; rep from *, end sl 3, k1.

Row 10—With B, k1, * sl 3 wyif, k2, p1, k2; rep from *, end sl 3, k1.

Row 11—With A, k6, * sl 1 wyib, k7; rep from *, end sl 1, k6.

Row 12—With A, k1, p5, * sl 1 wyif, p7; rep from *, end sl 1, p5, k1.

Rows 13, 14, and 15—Repeat Rows 9, 10, and 11.

Row 16—With A, repeat Row 8.

Repeat Rows 1–16.

Tile Pattern

Tile Pattern

This pattern utilizes some rather novel knitting techniques. Elongated slip-stitches are carried two stitches over on the diagonal, giving a roughly octagonal shape to the "tiles". Although each of these octagonal shapes is spanned by four rows of contrasting color in the center, the contrasting color is minimized into four little dots arranged in a square. The quilted effect of a Tile Pattern fabric makes it excellent for heavy ski sweaters, cushions, and hats. The fabric is dense; be sure to cast on enough stitches for width.

Multiple of 12 sts plus 1. Colors A and B.

Cast on with Color A and purl one row.

Row 1 (Preparation row—right side)—With B, k3, * sl 2 wyib, k1, sl 1 wyib, k1, sl 2 wyib, k5; rep from *, end last rep k3.

Row 2—With B, p3, * sl 2 wyif, k1, sl 1 wyif, k1, sl 2 wyif, p5; rep from *, end last rep p3.

Row 3—With A, k1, * sl 2 wyib, k7, sl 2 wyib, k1; rep from *.

Row 4—With A, k1, * sl 2 wyif, p7, sl 2 wyif, k1; rep from *.

Row 5—With B, k3, * sl 2 wyib, k1, sl 1 wyib, k1, sl 2 wyib, k5; rep from *, end last rep k3.

Row 6—With B, p2, * p1 wrapping yarn twice around needle, sl 2 wyif, k1, sl 1 wyif, k1, sl 2 wyif, p1 wrapping yarn twice, p3; rep from *, end last rep p2.

Row 7—With A, k2, * sl 1 wyib dropping extra wrap, k7, sl 1 wyib dropping extra wrap, k3; rep from *, end last rep k2.

Row 8—With A, p2, * sl 1 wyif, p7, sl 1 wyif, p3; rep from *, end last rep p2.

Row 9—With B, k2, * drop next sl-st off needle to front of work, sl 2 wyib, pick up dropped st and knit it, k3, sl 2 wyib, drop next sl-st off needle to front of work, sl the same 2 sts back to left-hand needle, pick up dropped st and knit it, sl 2 wyib (the same 2 sts that were slipped before), k1, sl 1 wyib, k1; rep from *, end last rep k2 instead of k1, sl 1, k1.

Row 10—With B, k2, * sl 2 wyif, p5, sl 2 wyif, k1, sl 1 wyif, k1; rep from *, end last rep k2 instead of k1, sl 1, k1.

Row 11—With A, k4, * sl 2 wyib, k1, sl 2 wyib, k7; rep from *, end last rep k4.

Row 12—With A, p4, * sl 2 wyif, k1, sl 2 wyif, p7; rep from *, end last rep p4.

Row 13—With B, k2, * sl 2 wyib, k5, sl 2 wyib, k1, sl 1 wyib, k1; rep from *, end last rep k2 instead of k1, sl 1, k1.

Row 14—With B, k2, * sl 2 wyif, p1 wrapping yarn twice around needle, p3, p1 wrapping yarn twice, sl 2 wyif, k1, sl 1 wyif, k1; rep from *, end last rep k2 instead of k1, sl 1, k1.

Row 15—With A, k4, * sl 1 wyib dropping extra wrap, k3, sl 1 wyib dropping extra wrap, k7; rep from *, end last rep k4.

Row 16—With A, p4, * sl 1 wyif, p3, sl 1 wyif, p7; rep from *, end last rep p4.

Row 17—With B, k2, * sl 2 wyib, drop next sl-st off needle to front of work, sl the same 2 sts back to left-hand needle, pick up dropped st and knit it, sl 2 wyib (the same 2 sts that were slipped before), k1, sl 1 wyib, k1, drop next sl-st off needle to front of work, sl 2 wyib, pick up dropped st and knit it, k3; rep from *, end last rep k2.

Omitting Row 1 from subsequent repeats, repeat Rows 2–17.

Dotted Block Pattern

Multiple of 7 sts plus 4. Colors A and B.

Row 1 (Wrong side)—With A, knit.

Row 2—With B, k1, * sl 2 wyib, k5; rep from *, end sl 2, k1.

Row 3—With B, k1, * sl 2 wyif, p5; rep from *, end sl 2, k1.

Row 4—With A, k3, * sl 2 wyib, k1, sl 2 wyib, k2; rep from *, end k1.

Row 5—With A, k1, * p2, sl 2 wyif, k1, sl 2 wyif; rep from *, end p2, k1.

Rows 6 and 7—With B, repeat Rows 2 and 3.

Row 8—With A, knit.

Repeat Rows 1–8.

Dotted Block Pattern

Diagonal Stripe

Diagonal Stripe

Multiple of 4 sts. Colors A and B.

Cast on with Color A and purl one row.

Row 1 (Right side)—With B, k1, * sl 2 wyib, k2; rep from *, end sl 2, k1.
Row 2—With B, k1, * sl 1 wyif, p3; rep from *, end sl 1, p1, k1.
Row 3—With A, k1, sl 1 wyib, * k2, sl 2 wyib; rep from *, end k2.
Row 4—With A, k1, p1, * sl 1 wyif, p3; rep from *, end sl 1, k1.
Row 5—With B, k1, * k2, sl 2 wyib; rep from *, end k3.
Row 6—With B, k1, p2, * sl 1 wyif, p3; rep from *, end k1.
Row 7—With A, * k2, sl 2 wyib; rep from *, end k2, sl 1, k1.
Row 8—With A, k1, * p3, sl 1 wyif; rep from *, end p2, k1.

Repeat Rows 1-8.

Dotted Diamond Pattern

Dotted Diamond Pattern

This is a really beautiful example of slip-stitch color knitting, a pattern that can make the simplest knitted garment wonderfully striking. A plain sweater, for instance, worked in this pattern, could surely be worn with pride.

Multiple of 20 sts plus 2. Colors A and B.

Cast on with Color A and purl one row.

NOTE: On right-side (odd-numbered) rows all sl-sts are slipped with yarn in back. On wrong-side (even-numbered) rows all sl-sts are slipped with yarn in front.

Row 1 (Right side)—With B, k1, * sl 1, k18, sl 1; rep from *, end k1.
Row 2—With B, k1, * sl 1, p18, sl 1; rep from *, end k1.
Row 3—With A, k1, * k3, sl 2, (k1, sl 1) twice, k2, (sl 1, k1) twice, sl 2, k3; rep from *, end k1.
Row 4—With A, k1, * p3, sl 2, (k1, sl 1) twice, k2, (sl 1, k1) twice, sl 2, p3; rep from *, end k1.
Row 5—With B, k1, * k1, sl 2, k14, sl 2, k1; rep from *, end k1.
Row 6—With B, k1, * p1, sl 2, p14, sl 2, p1; rep from *, end k1.
Row 7—With A, k1, * sl 1, k4, sl 2, k1, sl 1, k2, sl 1, k1, sl 2, k4, sl 1; rep from *, end k1.
Row 8—With A, k1, * sl 1, p4, sl 2, k1, sl 1, k2, sl 1, k1, sl 2, p4, sl 1; rep from *, end k1.
Row 9—With B, k1, * k3, sl 2, k10, sl 2, k3; rep from *, end k1.
Row 10—With B, k1, * p3, sl 2, p10, sl 2, p3; rep from *, end k1.
Row 11—With A, k1, * k1, sl 2, k4, sl 2, k2, sl 2, k4, sl 2, k1; rep from *, end k1.

Row 12—With A, k1, * k1, sl 2, p4, sl 2, k2, sl 2, p4, sl 2, k1; rep from *, end k1.

Row 13—With B, k1, * k5, sl 2, k6, sl 2, k5; rep from *, end k1.

Row 14—With B, k1, * p5, sl 2, p6, sl 2, p5; rep from *, end k1.

Row 15—With A, k1, * k1, sl 1, k1, sl 2, (k4, sl 2) twice, k1, sl 1, k1; rep from *, end k1.

Row 16—With A, k1, * k1, sl 1, k1, sl 2, (p4, sl 2) twice, k1, sl 1, k1; rep from *, end k1.

Row 17—With B, k1, * k7, sl 2, k2, sl 2, k7; rep from *, end k1.

Row 18—With B, k1, * p7, sl 2, p2, sl 2, p7; rep from *, end k1.

Row 19—With A, k1. * (k1, sl 1) twice, k1, sl 2, k6, sl 2, k1, (sl 1, k1) twice; rep from *, end k1.

Row 20—With A, k1, * (k1, sl 1) twice, k1, sl 2, p6, sl 2, k1, (sl 1, k1) twice; rep from *, end k1.

Row 21—With B, k1, * k9, sl 2, k9; rep from *, end k1.

Row 22—With B, k1, * p9, sl 2, p9; rep from *, end k1.

Rows 23 and 24—With A, repeat Rows 19 and 20.

Rows 25 and 26—With B, repeat Rows 17 and 18.

Rows 27 and 28—With A, repeat Rows 15 and 16.

Rows 29 and 30—With B, repeat Rows 13 and 14.

Rows 31 and 32—With A, repeat Rows 11 and 12.

Rows 33 and 34—With B, repeat Rows 9 and 10.

Rows 35 and 36—With A, repeat Rows 7 and 8.

Rows 37 and 38—With B, repeat Rows 5 and 6.

Rows 39 and 40—With A, repeat Rows 3 and 4.

Repeat Rows 1–40.

Cross-Color Stripe

This pattern may be worked in a straight stockinette version by purling all the stitches that are worked on Rows 2 and 4, slipping the slip-stitches with yarn in front as given. Or, it may be worked in a garter stitch version by knitting these same wrong-side stitches.

Multiple of 14 sts plus 9. Colors A and B.

Cast on with Color A and knit one row.

Row 1 (Right side)—With B, k1, * sl 1 wyib, k5, (sl 1 wyib, k3) twice; rep from *, end sl 1, k5, sl 1, k1.

Row 2—With B, k1, * sl 1 wyif, k5, (sl 1 wyif, p3) twice; rep from *, end sl 1, k5, sl 1, k1.

Row 3—With A, k1, * (k3, sl 1 wyib) twice, k5, sl 1 wyib; rep from *, end k3, sl 1, k4.

Row 4—With A, k1, * (p3, sl 1 wyif) twice, k5, sl 1 wyif; rep from *, end p3, sl 1, p3, k1.

Repeat Rows 1–4.

Cross-Color Stripe

Windows

This is a handsome arrangement of a check pattern into columns and bands, the checks being grouped into windows of six "panes" each. The pattern is wonderfully simple to work, and yet novel enough to make a most original garment.

Multiple of 10 sts plus 3. Colors A and B.

Row 1 (Right side)—With A, knit.
Row 2—With A, purl.
Row 3—With B, k1, sl 2 wyib, * k3, sl 1 wyib, k3, sl 3 wyib; rep from *, end last rep sl 2, k1.
Row 4—With B, k1, sl 2 wyif, * p3, sl 1 wyif, p3, sl 3 wyif; rep from *, end last rep sl 2, k1.
Row 5—With A, knit.
Row 6—With A, k1, p2, * k7, p3; rep from *, end last rep p2, k1.
Rows 7, 8, 9, 10, 11, and 12—Repeat Rows 3, 4, 5, and 6, then repeat Rows 3 and 4 once more.
Rows 13, 14, 15, and 16—With A, repeat Rows 1 and 2 twice.
Rows 17 and 18—With B, knit.
Rows 19 and 20—With A, repeat Rows 1 and 2.

Repeat Rows 1–20.

Windows

Harlequin Pattern

Here is a delightful pattern of contrasting diamonds with a nubby garter-stitch texture like that of a Waffle Check or Three-and-One Tweed. The same pattern may be given a smooth texture, if desired, simply by purling the wrong-side rows. Nubby or smooth, Harlequin Pattern is an excellent design for socks, knitted vests, or ties.

Multiple of 10 sts plus 3. Colors A and B.

Cast on with Color A and knit one row.

Note: On right-side (odd-numbered) rows slip all sl-sts with yarn in *back*.

Row 1 (Right side)—With B, k1, * sl 1, k9; rep from *, end sl 1, k1.
Row 2 and all other wrong-side rows—Using same color as previous row, repeat the previous row, but slip all sl-sts with yarn in *front*.
Row 3—With A, k3, * (sl 1, k1) 3 times, sl 1, k3; rep from *.
Row 5—With B, k2, * sl 1, k7, sl 1, k1; rep from *, end k1.
Row 7—With A, k4, * (sl 1, k1) twice, sl 1, k5; rep from *, end last repeat k4.

Harlequin Pattern

BLACK FOREST PATTERN
Directions on page 9

CARROUSEL CHECK
Directions on page 9

AMERICAN BEAUTY TWEED
Directions on page 10

DOUBLE TWIST CHECK
Directions on page 80

FOUR-COLOR MIX
Directions on page 21

SHERWOOD PATTERN
Directions on page 21

DICE CHECK
Directions on page 22

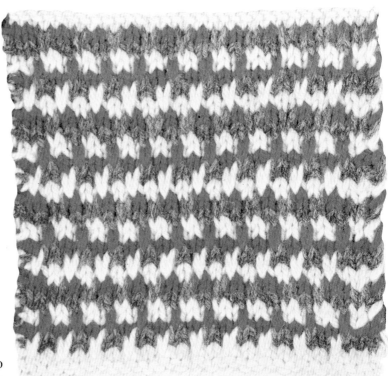

SYNCOPATED TWEED
Directions on page 22

OUTLINED CHECK PATTERN
Directions on page 29

HAYSTACK STRIPE
Directions on page 29

FOUR-COLOR PROGRESSIVE TWEED
Directions on page 30

STRIPED CHECK PATTERN
Directions on page 35

FOUR-COLOR FANCY PATTERN
Directions on page 35

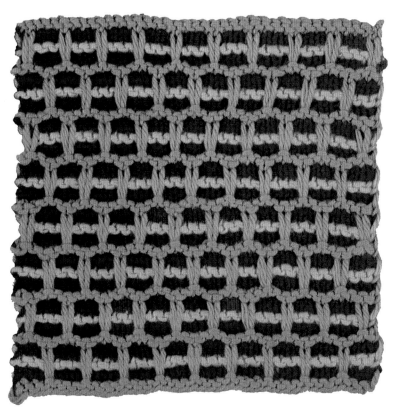

FANCY BRICKS
Directions on page 50

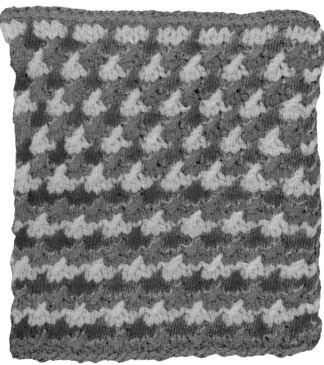

FINGERTIP TWEED
ABOVE: Check Version
BELOW: Stripe Version
Directions on page 80

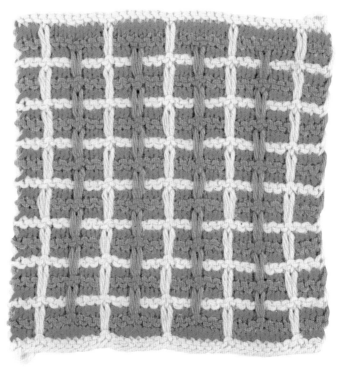

TRICOLOR BASKET PLAID
Directions on page 50

NAVAJO BASKET
Directions on page 51

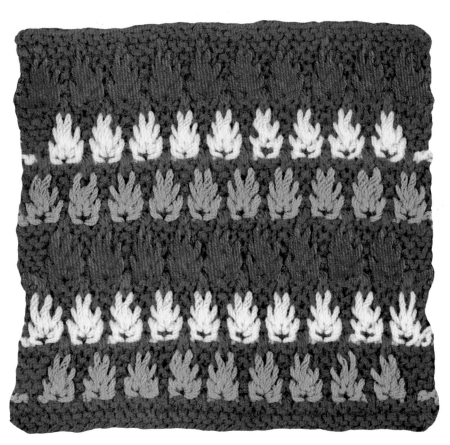

FIREFLOWERS
Directions on page 73

SCRAP-YARN AFGHAN STITCH
Directions on page 74

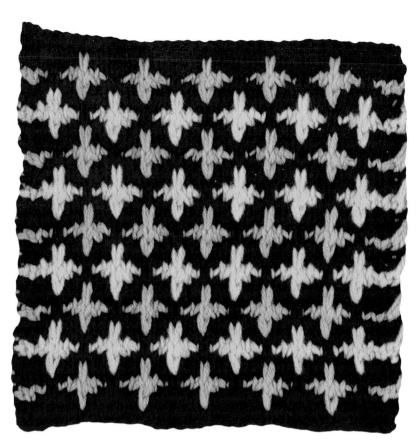

NORTH STAR PATTERN
Directions on page 77

COUNTERPOINT QUILTING
Directions on page 81

SUNRISE SHELL PATTERN
Directions on page 84

CACTUS FLOWER
Directions on page 81

ENGLISH ROSE TWEED
Directions on page 85

THREE-COLOR DAISY STITCH
Directions on page 85

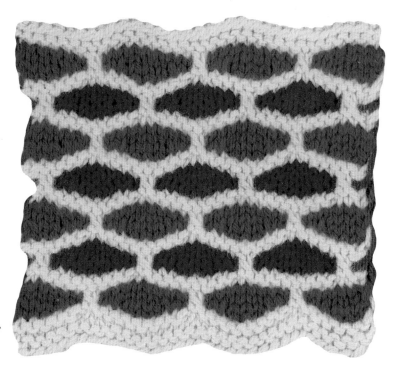

BONBON PATTERN
Directions on page 88

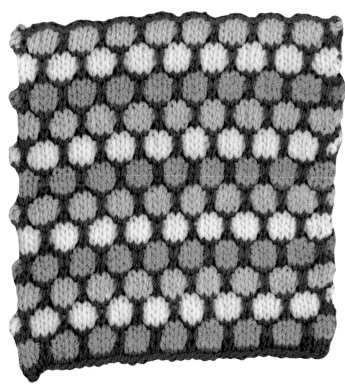

FOUR-COLOR BLISTER STITCH
Directions on page 88

THREE FLOWERS
Directions on page 89

Row 9—With B, (k1, sl 1) twice, * k5, (sl 1, k1) twice, sl 1; rep from *, end k5, (sl 1, k1) twice.

Row 11—With A, k5, * sl 1, k1, sl 1, k7; rep from *, end last repeat k5.

Row 13—With B, k1, (k1, sl 1) twice, * k3, (sl 1, k1) 3 times, sl 1; rep from *, end k3, (sl 1, k1) twice, k1.

Row 15—With A, k6, * sl 1, k9; rep from *, end last repeat k6.

Rows 17 and 18—With B, repeat Rows 13 and 14.

Rows 19 and 20—With A, repeat Rows 11 and 12.

Rows 21 and 22—With B, repeat Rows 9 and 10.

Rows 23 and 24—With A, repeat Rows 7 and 8.

Rows 25 and 26—With B, repeat Rows 5 and 6.

Rows 27 and 28—With A, repeat Rows 3 and 4.

Repeat Rows 1–28.

Sanquar Check

This is a slip-stitch imitation of the traditional Scottish Sanquar Pattern, which consists of plain light-colored squares alternating with dark-colored squares containing light accents. The original pattern is worked by the usual "Fair Isle" method of color knitting, and the squares are considerably larger than those in this slip-stitch version. Sanquar Check is, however, a crisp and handsome pattern, easy to work, and making a firm, flat fabric.

Sanquar Check

Multiple of 8 sts plus 3. Colors A and B.

Row 1 (Right side)—With A, knit.

Row 2—With A, knit.

Row 3—With B, k3, * (sl 1 wyib, k1) twice, sl 1 wyib, k3; rep from *.

Row 4—With B, p3, * (sl 1 wyif, k1) twice, sl 1 wyif, p3; rep from *.

Row 5—With A, k1, sl 2 wyib, * k5, sl 3 wyib; rep from *, end k5, sl 2, k1.

Row 6—With A, k1, sl 2 wyif, * k5, sl 3 wyif; rep from *, end k5, sl 2, k1.

Rows 7 and 8—With B, repeat Rows 3 and 4.

Rows 9 and 10—With A, repeat Rows 1 and 2.

Row 11—With B, (k1, sl 1 wyib) twice, * k3, (sl 1 wyib, k1) twice, sl 1 wyib; rep from *, end k3, (sl 1, k1) twice.

Row 12—With B, (k1, sl 1 wyif) twice, * p3, (sl 1 wyif, k1) twice, sl 1 wyif; rep from *, end p3, (sl 1, k1) twice.

Row 13—With A, k4, * sl 3 wyib, k5; rep from *, end last rep k4.

Row 14—With A, k4, * sl 3 wyif, k5; rep from *, end last rep k4.

Rows 15 and 16—With B, repeat Rows 11 and 12.

Repeat Rows 1–16.

Swiss Check

This is an extremely pretty pattern, simple to work, yet having some unusual features. Unlike most other slip-stitch color patterns, Swiss Check works different groups of stitches on the return row of the same color. The result is a very dainty check arranged diagonally in a lattice-like pattern. Be sure to keep yarn stranded *loosely* behind each group of three slipped stitches in Rows 2 and 6.

Swiss Check

Multiple of 4 sts plus 1. Colors A and B.

Row 1 (Wrong side)—With A, purl.
Row 2—With B, k1, sl 1 wyib, * k1, sl 3 wyib; rep from *, end k1, sl 1, k1.
Row 3—With B, k1, * p3, sl 1 wyif; rep from *, end p3, k1.
Row 4—With A, k2, * sl 1 wyib, k3; rep from *, end sl 1, k2.
Row 5—With A, purl.
Row 6—With B, k1, * sl 3 wyib, k1; rep from *.
Row 7—With B, k1, p1, * sl 1 wyif, p3; rep from *, end sl 1, p1, k1.
Row 8—With A, k4, * sl 1 wyib, k3; rep from *, end k1.

Repeat Rows 1–8.

Windowpane Stripes

Windowpane Stripes

A two-color version of the Stripe and Spot Pattern.

Odd number of sts. Colors A and B.

Cast on with Color B.

Row 1 (Right side)—With A, k1, * sl 1 wyib, k1; rep from *.
Row 2—With A, p1, * sl 1 wyif, p1; rep from *.
Rows 3 and 4—With B, knit.
Rows 5 and 6—With A, knit.
Rows 7 and 8—With B, knit.

Repeat Rows 1–8.

Fancy Color Patterns

This is a group of truly fascinating patterns. Some of them employ slip-stitches, but other knitting techniques are used as well: yarn-overs, short rows, bobbles, dip stitches, passed stitches—almost anything. These are Fancy Texture Patterns in color.

This section constitutes a demonstration of the enormous number of things that can be done with strands of two or three different colors and assorted knitting techniques. There are beautiful and unusual shapes here, which are enhanced by the interplay of light and dark, bright and subtle shades. Color work often seems to bring out the best of the pattern designer's ingenuity. Much variety is possible, too, in the use of color within the same pattern; this is for *you* to discover. If Color A happens to be a light color, and Color B a dark one, reverse them and see how different the pattern looks! Or try the same pattern, first with two strongly contrasting colors and then with two subtle ones, or with two shades of the same color.

You can do a lot of exciting things with these patterns, and use up a lot of old odds and ends of leftover yarn in trying them out. And when you have collected a large number of "test swatches" in all the colors of the rainbow and then some, sew them all together. The result will be the most glorious afghan you ever saw! You don't have to worry about working to a specific gauge in your test swatches, either. If they come out in several different sizes, just make a paper square the size of the smallest, place the square on each of the larger swatches, mark around its edge, and machine-stitch on the marks, twice around. Then you can cut off the excess from the larger squares without fear of raveling the knitting, and when they are sewn together (which is easily done, now that all are uniform in size and shape) the machine-stitching is concealed.

So—take out that old box of odd ounces and half-ounces of this and that—pick up your needles—and have fun.

Checked Rose Fabric

Checked Rose Fabric

This pattern makes a soft, deep texture with a good deal of lateral spread. Cast on and bind off very loosely, measure carefully, and beware of starting with too many stitches.

SPECIAL NOTE: This pattern must be worked back and forth on a circular needle or a pair of double-pointed needles.

Odd number of sts. Colors A and B.

Cast on with B and knit one row.

Row 1 (Wrong side)—With A, k1, * knit next st in the row below, k1; rep from *.
Row 2—With A, knit first st in the row below, * k1, knit next st in the row below; rep from *.
Row 3—With B, repeat Row 1.
Row 4—Sl all sts to other end of needle and with A, repeat Row 2.
Row 5—With A, repeat Row 1.
Row 6—Sl all sts to other end of needle and with B, repeat Row 2.

Repeat Rows 1–6.

Rickrack Stripe

Contributed by Hildegard M. Elsner, Aldan, Pennsylvania

Either version of this pattern is beautiful in three colors. Continue to alternate the three colors, allotting 2 pattern rows to each color. The wrong side of this fabric is very interesting also.

Even number of sts. Colors A and B.

Cast on with Color A and purl one row.

Row 1 (Right side)—With B, k1, * skip 1 st and insert needle from front into the st *in the row below* the 2nd st on left-hand needle; draw through a loop, sl the loop onto left-hand needle and knit it together with the skipped st through *back* loops; k1; rep from *, end k1.
Row 2—With B, purl.
Rows 3 and 4—With A, repeat Rows 1 and 2.

Repeat Rows 1–4.

VARIATION: *ALTERNATING RICKRACK STRIPE*

Work the same as above, with the following exception:

Row 3—With A, k2, rep from * of Row 1, end k2.

ABOVE: *Rickrack Stripe*
BELOW: *Alternating Rickrack Stripe*

Leaning Stripe Pattern

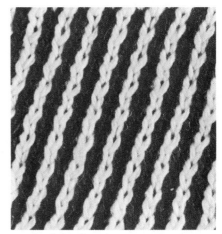

Multiple of 3 sts. Colors A and B.

Cast on with Color A.

NOTE: Right Twist (RT)—Skip 1 st and knit into 2nd st, then knit the skipped st, then sl both sts from needle together.

Preparation Row (Right side)—With B, * k2, sl 1 wyib; rep from *, end k3.
Row 1—With B, p3, * sl 1 wyif, p2; rep from *.
Row 2—With A, k1, * RT, sl 1 wyib; rep from *, end k2.
Row 3—With A, * p2, sl 1 wyif; rep from *, end p3.
Row 4—With B, k1, * sl 1 wyib, RT; rep from *, end sl 1, k1.
Row 5—With B, p1, * sl 1 wyif, p2; rep from *, end sl 1, p1.
Row 6—With A, * RT, sl 1 wyib; rep from *, end RT, k1.
Rows 7 through 12—Repeat Rows 1 through 6, reversing colors.

Repeat Rows 1–12.

Leaning Stripe Pattern

Swedish Weave

In this pattern Color B is never worked, only passed back and forth between the needles as the knitting is done with Color A. The Color B strand need not be held in the fingers at all, but simply pushed from front to back as required. In this way the strand is kept quite loose, which gives the best results. The fabric has an unusually beautiful purl side.

Odd number of sts. Colors A and B.

Cast on with Color A and purl one row. Join Color B.

Row 1 (Right side)—k1 Color A st, passing Color B strand across st at front of work; * pass Color B strand to back between needles and knit next Color A st with B in back; pass Color B strand to front between needles and knit next Color A st with B in front; rep from *.

Row 2—P1 Color A st and bring Color B strand around edge to pass in front (i.e., on the wrong side of work) of purl st; * pass Color B strand to back between needles and purl next Color A st with B in back; pass Color B strand to front between needles and purl next Color A st with B in front; rep from *.

Repeat Rows 1 and 2.

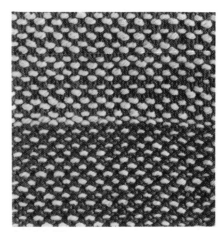

Swedish Weave
ABOVE: *knit side*
BELOW: *purl side*

Two "Turning" Patterns: String of Purls and Short-Row Pattern

Both of these unusual patterns are made by turning the work around and working back over the most recent stitches, after the manner of a bobble. The Short-Row Pattern picks up two extra stitches at each end of a "turned" row, so that the motif spreads out into a sort of upside-down pyramid.

ABOVE: *String of Purls*
BELOW: *Short-Row Pattern*

I. STRING OF PURLS

Multiple of 12 sts. Colors A and B.

Rows 1 and 3 (Wrong side)—With A, purl.
Row 2—With A, knit.
Row 4—With B, k11, * turn; sl 1 wyif, k3, turn; p4, k12; rep from *, end last repeat k1 instead of k12.
Row 5—With B, k5, * turn; p4, turn; k3, sl 1 wyif, k12; rep from *, end last repeat k7 instead of k12.
Row 6—With A, k8, * sl 2 wyib, k10; rep from *, end last repeat k2 instead of k10.
Rows 7, 8, and 9—With A, repeat Rows 1, 2, and 3.
Row 10—With B, k5, * turn; sl 1 wyif, k3, turn; p4, k12; rep from *, end last repeat k7 instead of k12.
Row 11—With B, k11, * turn; p4, turn; k3, sl 1 wyif, k12; rep from *, end last repeat k1 instead of k12.
Row 12—With A, k2, * sl 2 wyib, k10; rep from *, end last repeat k8 instead of k10.

Repeat Rows 1–12.

II. SHORT-ROW PATTERN

Multiple of 22 sts plus 4. Colors A and B.

Rows 1 and 3 (Right side)—With A, knit.
Rows 2 and 4—With A, purl.
Row 5—With B, k2, * k7, turn; sl 1 wyif, p2, turn; sl 1 wyib, k4, turn; sl 1 wyif, p6, turn; sl 1 wyib, k8, turn; sl 1 wyif, p10, turn; sl 1 wyib, k21; rep from *, end k2.
Row 6—With B, k2, * k11, p11; rep from *, end k2.
Rows 7 through 10—With A, repeat Rows 1 through 4.
Row 11—With B, k13, rep from * of Row 5, end last repeat k12 instead of k21.
Row 12—With B, k2, * p11, k11; rep from *, end k2.

Repeat Rows 1–12.

Fancy Shingle Pattern

This pattern produces overlapping "shingles" that are raised at the lower edges and decorated with scalloped borders of Color A. The method of avoiding holes on the turning rows is the same as that used by knowledgeable knitters in garment shaping, such as the short rows on shoulders or collars: i.e., "hooking" the yarn around an unworked stitch before turning the work. By trying the pattern both with and without this little trick, the novice knitter can prove its advantages for herself.

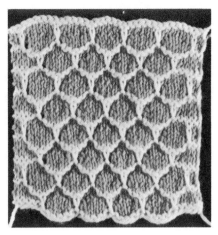

Fancy Shingle Pattern

Multiple of 6 sts plus 3. Colors A and B.

Row 1 (Wrong side)—With A, knit.
Row 2—With B, k4, * sl 1 wyib, k5; turn; sl 1 wyif, p4; turn; sl 1 wyib, k4; turn; sl 1 wyif, p4; then sl the next (Color A) st wyif, sl the following st wyib; bring yarn through to front (i.e., wrong side of work), then sl the last 2 sts back again to left-hand needle; turn; sl 1 wyib, k4; rep from *, end sl 1 wyib, k4.
Row 3—With B, p4, * sl 1 wyif, p5; rep from *, end sl 1, p4.
Row 4—With A, k4, * k1-b, k5; rep from *, end k1-b, k4.
Row 5—With A, knit.
Row 6—With B, k1, rep from * of Row 2; end sl 1 wyib, k1.
Row 7—With B, p1, * sl 1 wyif, p5; rep from *, end sl 1, p1.
Row 8—With A, k1, * k1-b, k5; rep from *, end k1-b, k1.

Repeat Rows 1–8.

Two-Color Star Stitch

This is a remarkably beautiful openwork pattern used for fancy baby clothes, yokes, dress sleeves, evening purses, cushions, place mats, and the like. It may be lined with a fabric matching one of the colors or with a contrasting color. It also looks well when done in ribbon, or a combination of ribbon and yarn.

Two-Color Star Stitch

Multiple of 3 sts. Colors A and B.

Row 1 (Wrong side)—With A, purl.
Row 2—With A, k2, * yo, k3, pass first of the 3 knit sts over the 2nd and 3rd sts; rep from *, end k1.
Row 3—With B, purl.
Row 4—With B, k1, * k3, pass first of the 3 knit sts over the 2nd and 3rd sts, yo; rep from *, end k2.

Repeat Rows 1–4.

Closed Star Stitch

Closed Star Stitch

Though the technique here is basically the same as the Two-Color Star Stitch, the yarn-over is replaced by a lifted increase from the wrong side, which makes a tighter fabric, more suitable to work in medium-weight and heavy yarns. This version is good for suits, jackets, and afghans.

Multiple of 3 sts plus 2. Colors A and B.

Cast on with A and purl one row.

Row 1 (Right side)—With A, k1, * k3, pass first of the 3 knit sts over the 2nd and 3rd sts; rep from *, end k1.

Row 2—With B, p1, * insert needle from behind under running thread between the st just worked and the next st, and purl this thread; p2; rep from *, end p1.

Row 3—With B, k2, rep from * of Row 1 across.

Row 4—With A, p2, rep from * of Row 2 across.

Repeat Rows 1–4.

Butterfly Quilting

Butterfly Quilting

It is particularly important in this pattern to keep the Color B strands *loose* as they are carried across the front of the fabric. The pattern will be spoiled if these strands are taut.

Multiple of 6 sts plus 3. Colors A and B.

Cast on with Color A and purl one row.

Row 1 (Right side)—With B, k2, * sl 5 wyif, k1; rep from *, end k1.

Row 2—With B, p2, * sl 5 wyib, p1; rep from *, end p1.

Row 3—With A, knit.

Row 4—With A, purl.

Row 5—With A, k4, * insert needle under the loose Color B strands and knit next st, catching both strands behind st as it is knitted; k5; rep from *, end last repeat k4.

Row 6—With A, purl.

Row 7—With B, k1, sl 3 wyif, * k1, sl 5 wyif; rep from *, end k1, sl 3 wyif, k1.

Row 8—With B, p1, sl 3 wyib, * p1, sl 5 wyib; rep from *, end p1, sl 3 wyib, p1.

Rows 9 and 10—With A, repeat Rows 3 and 4.

Row 11—With A, k1, * insert needle under the loose Color B strands and knit next st, k5; rep from *, end last repeat k1.

Row 12—With A, purl.

Repeat Rows 1–12.

Fireflowers *See color page x*

This is a 20-row pattern, with the extra rows serving only to alternate colors. It may be worked in three colors only—one for the background, two for the pattern stripes—by repeating just Rows 1–20. Or it may be worked in two colors, using B for Rows 11 and 12 as well as 1 and 2. In this four-color version, it is best to break the strands of B, C, and D after the second and twelfth rows, rather than carrying them up the side of the piece, because it is a long stretch before these colors are repeated.

The "ssk" (which involves one long stitch and one background stitch) at the left-hand sides of the flowers must be worked correctly for best results. Be sure you slip both stitches *knitwise* before knitting them together; for if the long stitch is slipped purlwise it will be twisted, and will spoil the shape of the flower. The strands should be quite loose.

This pattern may be used in one, two, or three repeats as a pretty border design.

Multiple of 4 sts plus 1. Colors A, B, C, and D.

Cast on with Color A and knit two rows.

Row 1 (Right side)—With B, k2, * sl 1 wyib, k1, (k1, yo, k1, yo, k1) in next st, k1; rep from *, end sl 1 wyib, k2.

Row 2—With B, k2, * sl 1 wyif, k1, p5 wrapping yarn twice for each st, k1; rep from *, end sl 1 wyif, k2.

Row 3—With A, k4, * sl 5 wyib dropping extra wraps, k3; rep from *, end k1.

Row 4—With A, k4, * sl 5 wyif, k3; rep from *, end k1.

Row 5—With A, k3, * k2 tog, sl 3 wyib, ssk, k1; rep from *, end k2.

Row 6—With A, k3, * p1, sl 3 wyif, p1, k1; rep from *, end k2.

Row 7—With A, k3, * k2 tog, sl 1 wyib, ssk, k1; rep from *, end k2.

Row 8—With A, k3, * p1, sl 1 wyif, p1, k1; rep from *, end k2.

Row 9—With A, k4, * k1-b, k3; rep from *, end k1.

Row 10—With A, k4, * p1-b, k3; rep from *, end k1.

Row 11—With C, k2, * (k1, yo, k1, yo, k1) in next st, k1, sl 1 wyib, k1; rep from *, end (k1, yo, k1, yo, k1) in next st, k2.

Row 12—With C, k2, * p5 wrapping yarn twice for each st, k1, sl 1 wyif, k1; rep from *, end p5 wrapping yarn twice for each st, k2.

Row 13—With A, k2, * sl 5 wyib dropping extra wraps, k3; rep from *, end last repeat k2.

Row 14—With A, k2, * sl 5 wyif, k3; rep from *, end last repeat k2.

Row 15—With A, k1, * k2 tog, sl 3 wyib, ssk, k1; rep from *.

Row 16—With A, k1, * p1, sl 3 wyif, p1, k1; rep from *.

Row 17—With A, k1, * k2 tog, sl 1 wyib, ssk, k1; rep from *.

Row 18—With A, k1, * p1, sl 1 wyif, p1, k1; rep from *.

Row 19—With A, k2, * k1-b, k3; rep from *, end last repeat k2.

Row 20—With A, k2, * p1-b, k3; rep from *, end last repeat k2.

Rows 21 and 22—With D, repeat Rows 1 and 2.

Rows 23 through 30—With A, repeat Rows 3 through 10.

Rows 31 and 32—With B, repeat Rows 11 and 12.
Rows 33 through 40—With A, repeat Rows 13 through 20.
Rows 41 and 42—With C, repeat Rows 1 and 2.
Rows 43 through 50—With A, repeat Rows 3 through 10.
Rows 51 and 52—With D, repeat Rows 11 and 12.
Rows 53 through 60—With A, repeat Rows 13 through 20.

Repeat Rows 1–60.

Scrap-Yarn Afghan Stitch See color page xi

Here is an excellent solution to every knitter's perennial problem: what to do with leftover yarn scraps. This easy-to-work pattern, knitted in strips of 63 or 75 stitches each, will produce a beautiful afghan that uses every little yarn-end in your scrap box—the more colors, the better. Strips can be sewn or crocheted together at the sides, either across the width or along the length of the afghan, as desired. The cast-on and bound-off edges of each strip will form a handsomely scalloped self-border.

Colors are worked two at a time and changed at will at the beginning of any right-side row. The illustration shows three stripes of each color, but you need not stick to this or any other system; random alternation of colors is effective too. This pattern is as flexible as your imagination. You may use all kinds of yarn in the same piece; single strands of the heavier ones, double or triple strands of the thinner ones.

When used with the same two or three colors throughout, the pattern makes a delightful scarf, lap robe, or baby blanket. A stockinette-stitch variation, given below, will make lovely sweaters and jackets with scalloped edges.

Multiple of 12 sts plus 3. Colors A and B.

Cast on with Color A and knit one row.

Row 1 (Right side)—With B, k1, ssk, * k9, sl 2—k1—p2sso; rep from *, end k9, k2 tog, k1.
Row 2—With B, k1, * p1, k4, (k1, yo, k1) in next st, k4; rep from *, end p1, k1.
Rows 3 and 4—With A, repeat Rows 1 and 2.

Repeat Rows 1–4.

STOCKINETTE-STITCH VARIATION
(*not illustrated*)

Rows 1 and 3—Same as above.
Rows 2 and 4—P6, * (p1, yo, p1) in next st, p9; rep from *, end last repeat p6.

Quilted Check

Multiple of 6 sts plus 2. Colors A and B.

Cast on with Color A and knit one row.

Row 1 (Wrong side)—With A, p1, * sl 3 wyib, p3; rep from *, end p1.
Row 2—With B, * k5, sl 1 wyif; rep from *, end k2.
Row 3—With B, p2, * sl 1 wyib, p5; rep from *.
Row 4—With A, * k5, insert left-hand needle down behind loose Color A strand of Row 1; lift this strand over point of left-hand needle and k2 tog-b (i.e., the Color A strand and the 1st Color B st on needle); rep from *, end k2.
Row 5—With A, p4, * sl 3 wyib, p3; rep from *, end sl 3, p1.
Row 6—With B, k2, * sl 1 wyif, k5; rep from *.
Row 7—With B, * p5, sl 1 wyib; rep from *, end p2.
Row 8—With A, k2, * insert left-hand needle under Color A strand of Row 5, and k2 tog-b, as in Row 4; k5; rep from *.

Repeat Rows 1–8.

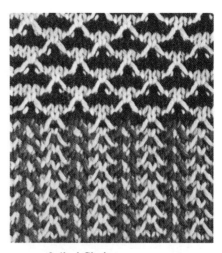

ABOVE: *Quilted Check*
BELOW: *Interlaced Stripe*

Interlaced Stripe

Contributed by Hildegard M. Elsner, Aldan, Pennsylvania

Multiple of 6 sts plus 2. Colors A and B.

PREPARATION ROWS

Row 1 (Right side)—With A, knit.
Row 2—With A, p1, * sl 3 wyib, p3; rep from *, end p1.
Row 3—With B, knit.

End of preparation rows.

Row 4—With B, p4, * sl 3 wyib, p3; rep from *, end sl 3, p1.
Row 5—With A, * k5, insert left-hand needle down behind loose Color A strand of Row 2; lift this strand over point of left-hand needle and k2 tog-b (i.e., the Color A strand and the 1st Color B st on needle); rep from *, end k2.
Row 6—With A, p1, * sl 3 wyib, p3; rep from *, end p1.
Row 7—With B, k2, * insert left-hand needle down behind loose Color B strand of Row 4, lift up and k2 tog-b, as in Row 5; k5; rep from *.

Omitting preparation rows, repeat Rows 4–7.

Plaited Diagonal Stripe

Plaited Diagonal Stripe

Each right-side row decreases one stitch in each pattern repeat, and each wrong-side row restores it by a yo. Since the fabric is quite dense laterally, it is a good idea to bind off on the wrong side *without* restoring the subtracted stitches; this will prevent the bind-off row from showing an unattractive "spread".

Multiple of 4 sts plus 2. Colors A and B.

Cast on with A and purl one row.

Row 1 (Right side)—With B, k1, * sl 1 wyib, k2, psso the 2 knit sts, sl 1 wyib; rep from *, end k1.
Row 2—With B, * p1, sl 1 wyif, p1, yo; rep from *, end p2.
Row 3—With A, k3, * sl 2 wyib, k2, pass the *second* sl-st over the 2 subsequent knit sts; rep from *, end sl 1, k2.
Row 4—With A, p2, * sl 1 wyif, p1, yo, p1; rep from * to last 4 sts, end sl 1, p3.
Row 5—With B, k2, * sl 2 wyib, k2, pass the *second* sl-st over the 2 subsequent knit sts; rep from * to last 4 sts, end sl 1, k3.
Row 6—With B, p3, * sl 1 wyif, p1, yo, p1; rep from *, end sl 1, p2.
Row 7—With A, k1, * sl 2 wyib, k2, pass the *second* sl-st over the 2 subsequent knit sts; rep from *, end k1.
Row 8—With A, p2, * yo, p1, sl 1 wyif, p1; rep from *.

Repeat Rows 1–8.

Thorn Pattern

Thorn Pattern

This pattern is simple to work, and creates a really beautiful fabric. The technique is ingenious and unusual, but no "acrobatic" knitting is required to accomplish it; on the contrary, it goes very quickly. The fabric is firm enough for suits and coats, though not truly heavy.

Multiple of 4 sts plus 1. Colors A and B.

Row 1 (Right side)—With A, k2, * (k1, yo, k1) in next st, k3; rep from *, end last repeat k2.
Row 2—With B, p2, * sl 3 wyif, p3; rep from *, end last repeat p2.
Row 3—With B, k1, * k2 tog, sl 1 wyib, ssk, k1; rep from *.
Row 4—With A, p4, * sl 1 wyif, p3; rep from *, end p1.
Row 5—With A, k4, * (k1, yo, k1) in next st, k3; rep from *, end k1.
Row 6—With B, p4, * sl 3 wyif, p3; rep from *, end p1.
Row 7—With B, k3, * k2 tog, sl 1 wyib, ssk, k1; rep from *, end k2.
Row 8—With A, p2, * sl 1 wyif, p3; rep from *, end last repeat p2.

Repeat Rows 1–8.

Three-and-One Tweed

This is the classic Three-and-One slip-stitch pattern worked in two colors.

Multiple of 4 sts plus 3. Colors A and B.

Cast on with Color B and knit one row.

Row 1 (Right side)—With A, k3, * sl 1 wyib, k3; rep from *.
Row 2—With A, k3, * sl 1 wyif, k3; rep from *.
Row 3—With B, k1, * sl 1 wyib, k3; rep from *, end sl 1, k1.
Row 4—With B, k1, * sl 1 wyif, k3; rep from *, end sl 1, k1.

Repeat Rows 1–4.

Three-and-One Tweed

North Star Pattern   *See color page xii*

Dip-stitches are used in this pretty design to make small cross-shaped or star-shaped motifs against a continuous background of Color A. Keep the yarn *loose* behind each group of three slipped stitches in Rows 5, 7, 11, and 13.

Multiple of 6 sts plus 5. Colors A, B, and C.

PREPARATION ROWS

Rows 1 and 3 (Right side)—With A, knit.
Rows 2 and 4—With A, purl.

End of preparation rows.

Row 5—With B, k1, * sl 3 wyib, k1, make dip st as follows: insert needle into front of st in the 3rd row below the next st on left-hand needle, and draw through a loose loop; sl loop onto left-hand needle and k2 tog-b (the loop and the next st)—dip st completed—k1; rep from *, end sl 3 wyib, k1.
Row 6—With B, p2, * sl 1 wyif, p5; rep from *, end sl 1, p2.
Row 7—With A, k4, * sl 3 wyib, k3; rep from *, end k1.
Row 8—With A, p5, * sl 1 wyif, p5; rep from *.
Row 9—With A, k5, * sl 1 wyib, k5; rep from *.
Row 10—With A, purl.
Row 11—With C, k2, * make dip st as in Row 5, k1, sl 3 wyib, k1; rep from *, end: make dip st, k2.
Row 12—With C, repeat Row 8.
Row 13—With A, k1, * sl 3 wyib, k3; rep from *, end sl 3, k1.
Row 14—With A, repeat Row 6.
Row 15—With A, k2, * sl 1 wyib, k5; rep from *, end sl 1, k2.
Row 16—With A, purl.

Omitting preparation rows, repeat Rows 5–16.

Chain of Triangles

Stitches are increased on the Color B rows in this pattern, and reduced to the original number again on the Color A rows. The variation, below, is a pretty "rib" design. Both versions are easy to work.

Multiple of 6 sts plus 3. Colors A and B.

Row 1 (Wrong side)—With A, k2, * p2, k1; rep from *, end k1.
Row 2—With B, k1, inc in next st, * sl 1 wyib, k3, sl 1 wyib, (k1, p1, k1) in next st; rep from *, end sl 1, k3, sl 1, inc in next st, k1.
Row 3—With B, p3, * sl 1 wyif, p3; rep from *.
Row 4—With A, k3, * ssk, sl 1 wyib, k2 tog, k3; rep from *.
Row 5—With A, k3, * p1, sl 1 wyif, p1, k3; rep from *.
Row 6—With B, k2, inc in next st, * (sl 1 wyib, k1) twice, (k1, p1, k1) in next st, k1; rep from *, end sl 1, k1, sl 1, inc in next st, k2.
Row 7—With B, p4, * sl 1 wyif, p1, sl 1 wyif, p5; rep from *, end last repeat p4.
Row 8—With A, k4, * sl 1—k2 tog—psso, k5; rep from *, end last repeat k4.

Repeat Rows 1–8.

VARIATION

Rows 1, 2, and 3—Same as rows 1, 2, and 3 above.
Row 4—With A, k3, * ssk, k1, k2 tog, k3; rep from *.

Repeat Rows 1–4.

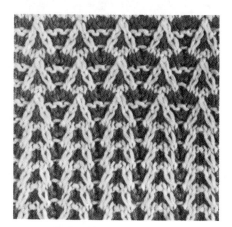

ABOVE: *Chain of Triangles*
BELOW: *Variation*

Two-Color Plaited Basketweave

On a purely physical basis, this pattern is not an easy one to work. It is *extremely* dense (a large number of stitches makes a surprisingly small piece) and should be worked with large needles. The dropped stitch may shorten so much that it is difficult to retrieve, especially in Row 2. But this awkwardness can be overcome by putting the stitch on a cable needle instead of simply dropping it. Some knitters will find one of these methods preferable, some the other. Notice that the third, or "extra" stitch in each pattern repeat is lost in the background as the fabric pulls together. This gives additional depth and thickness to the knitting, making a fabric so tough and durable that it would even serve as a rug.

Two-Color Plaited Basketweave

Multiple of 3 sts. Colors A and B.

Cast on with Color A and knit one row.

Row 1 (Wrong side)—With B, p3, * sl 1 wyif, p2; rep from *.

Row 2—With B, k2, * drop next (Color A) st off needle to front of work, k2, then with point of left-hand needle pick up dropped st and slip it onto right-hand needle without working; rep from *, end k1.

Row 3—With A, * p2, sl 1 wyif; rep from *, end p3.

Row 4—With A, k1, * sl 2 wyib, drop next (Color B) st off needle to front of work, sl the same 2 sts back to left-hand needle, pick up dropped st onto right-hand needle without working, k2; rep from *, end k2.

Repeat Rows 1–4.

False Flame Stitch

Here is a knitted imitation of the Flame Stitch, or Bargello Pattern. It may be worked in three or four colors if desired, simply by repeating the 4 pattern rows for each stripe of color. It is very handsome in a progressive series of colors, such as: white, yellow, orange, red; or: white, light gray, dark gray, black. The 3 Preparation Rows are always worked in the last color to be used.

Multiple of 4 sts plus 1. Colors A and B.

PREPARATION ROWS:

Row 1 (Wrong side)—With A, purl.

Row 2—With A, knit.

Row 3—With A, p2, * p1 wrapping yarn twice, p3; rep from *, end last repeat p2.

End of preparation rows.

False Flame Stitch

Row 4—With B, k2, * sl 1 wyib dropping extra wrap, k1, insert needle into next st 2 rows below and draw through a loop loosely; knit next st and pass the loop over the st just knitted; k1; rep from *, end sl 1 wyib, k2.

Row 5—With B, p2, * sl 1 wyif, p3; rep from *, end sl 1 wyif, p2.

Row 6—With B, knit.

Row 7—With B, p2, * p1 wrapping yarn twice, p3; rep from *, end last repeat p2.

Rows 8 through 11—With A, repeat Rows 4 through 7.

Omitting preparation rows, repeat Rows 4–11.

Double Twist Check *See color page ii*

Multiple of 6 sts plus 3. Colors A, B, and C.

Row 1 (Wrong side)—With A, purl.
Row 2—With B, k1, * k4, sl 2 wyib; rep from *, end k2.
Row 3—With B, p2, * sl 2 wyif, p4; rep from *, end p1.
Row 4—With A, k2, * sl 2 wyib, RT, LT; rep from *, end k1.
Row 5—With A, purl.
Row 6—With C, k2, * sl 2 wyib, k4; rep from *, end k1.
Row 7—With C, p1, * p4, sl 2 wyif; rep from *, end p2.
Row 8—With A, k1, * RT, LT, sl 2 wyib; rep from *, end k2.

Repeat Rows 1–8.

Fingertip Tweed *See color page viii*

In Version I of this pattern, the middle stitch of the 3 knit stitches (which is the slipped stitch of the previous row) presents the back loop, so it is somewhat easier to work it as a "k1-b" than as a plain knit stitch. This action produces a third variation, which is not shown; the knitter may try it, and see what it looks like. Knitting this middle stitch in its front loop, in spite of the way it is turned, makes the twisted diagonal point above each check; so be sure to do this if you want your sample to look like the illustration. This distinction does not exist, of course, in Version II.

Multiple of 4 sts plus 3. Colors A, B, and C.

Cast on with Color C.

I. CHECK VERSION

Row 1 (Right side)—With A, k3, * skip 1 st and insert needle purlwise into the front of 2nd st, then slip this st *over* skipped st onto right-hand needle (leaving skipped st in place); k3; rep from *.
Row 2—With A, p3, * sl 1 wyif, p3; rep from *.
Row 3—With B, k1, rep from * of Row 1; end last repeat k1 instead of k3.
Row 4—With B, p1, * sl 1 wyif, p3; rep from *, end sl 1, p1.
Rows 5 and 6—With C, repeat Rows 1 and 2.
Rows 7 and 8—With A, repeat Rows 3 and 4.
Rows 9 and 10—With B, repeat Rows 1 and 2.
Rows 11 and 12—With C, repeat Rows 3 and 4.

Repeat Rows 1–12.

II. STRIPE VERSION

Work the same as I, above, except: *purl* all sts on all wrong-side rows.

Cactus Flower   *See color page xiii*

Though done with a technique similar to that of Counterpoint Quilting, this pattern has quite a different appearance. On Rows 2 and 8, the strand should be kept *loose* behind the three slipped stitches, as this is the strand that will be picked up later (Rows 5 and 11). Widely varying effects can be had from this pattern by alternating light and dark, bright and dull colors on different rows.

Multiple of 6 sts plus 5. Colors A, B, and C.

Cast on with Color A and purl one row.

Row 1 (Right side)—With B, k2, * sl 1 wyib, k5; rep from *, end sl 1, k2.
Row 2—With B, p4, * sl 3 wyib, p3; rep from *, end p1.
Row 3—With C, k1, * sl 1 wyib, k1, sl 1 wyib, k3; rep from *, end (sl 1, k1) twice.
Row 4—With C, purl.
Row 5—With A, k1, * sl 3 wyib, k1, insert needle under the loose Color B strand on front of fabric and knit next st, catching strand behind st; k1; rep from *, end sl 3, k1.
Row 6—With A, p2, * sl 1 wyif, p5; rep from *, end sl 1, p2.
Row 7—With B, k5, * sl 1 wyib, k5; rep from *.
Row 8—With B, p1, * sl 3 wyib, p3; rep from *, end sl 3, p1.
Row 9—With C, k4, * sl 1 wyib, k1, sl 1 wyib, k3; rep from *, end k1.
Row 10—With C, purl.
Row 11—With A, k2, * knit next st under loose Color B strand (as in Row 5), k1, sl 3 wyib, k1; rep from *, end knit next st under loose strand, k2.
Row 12—With A, p5, * sl 1 wyif, p5; rep from *.

Repeat Rows 1–12.

Counterpoint Quilting   *See color page xii*

Contributed by Hildegard M. Elsner, Aldan, Pennsylvania

Multiple of 6 sts plus 5. Colors A, B, and C.

Row 1 (Wrong side)—With A, p4, * sl 3 wyib, p3; rep from *, end p1.
Row 2—With B, knit.
Row 3—With B, repeat Row 1.
Rows 4 and 5—With C, repeat Rows 2 and 3.
Row 6—With A, k5, * insert needle from front under the 3 loose strands and upward to knit next st, catching all 3 strands behind st as it is knitted; k5; rep from *.
Row 7—With A, p1, * sl 3 wyib, p3; rep from *, end last repeat p1.
Row 8—With B, knit.
Row 9—With B, repeat Row 7.
Rows 10 and 11—With C, repeat Rows 8 and 9.
Row 12—With A, k2, rep from * of Row 6; end last repeat k2 instead of k5.

Repeat Rows 1–12.

Fancy Diagonal Stripe

This pattern is an elaboration of Plaited Diagonal Stripe, done with a similar technique, and should be bound off in the same way (i.e., on the wrong side, omitting all yo's) for the same reason. Although the basis of the two patterns is the same, the general effect is quite different; this one is decidedly more complex, both in appearance and in construction. Note that in this pattern the slip-stitches are sometimes single, sometimes double; when they are double, it is always the *second* of the two slipped stitches that is passed over two subsequent knit stitches. The wrong side of this fabric shows a very interesting diagonal stripe in purl and slipped stitches. For a test swatch, cast on a *minimum* of 18 sts.

Fancy Diagonal Stripe

Multiple of 8 sts plus 2. Colors A and B.

Cast on with A and purl one row.

NOTE: On all right-side (odd-numbered) rows sl all sl-sts with yarn in back; on all wrong-side (even-numbered) rows sl all sl-sts with yarn in front.

Row 1 (Right side)—With B, k2, * sl 1, k2, psso the 2 knit sts, sl 2, k2, pass 2nd sl-st over the 2 knit sts, k1; rep from *.

Row 2—With B, p2, * yo, p1, sl 1, p1, yo, p3; rep from *.

Row 3—With A, k1, * sl 1, k2, psso the 2 knit sts, k1, sl 1, k2, psso the 2 knit sts, sl 1; rep from *, end k1.

Row 4—With A, p1, * sl 1, p1, yo, p3, yo, p1; rep from *, end p1.

Row 5—With B, k3, * sl 2, k2, pass 2nd sl-st over the 2 knit sts, k1, sl 1, k2, psso the 2 knit sts; rep from *, end sl 2, k2, pass 2nd sl-st over the 2 knit sts, k3.

Row 6—With B, p4, * yo, p1, sl 1, p1, yo, p3; rep from *, end yo, p1, sl 1, p3.

Row 7—With A, k3, * sl 1, k2, psso the 2 knit sts, sl 2, k2, pass 2nd sl-st over the 2 knit sts, k1; rep from *, omitting final "k1" from last repeat.

Row 8—With A, p1, * yo, p1, sl 1, p1, yo, p3; rep from *, end p1.

Row 9—With B, k1, * sl 2, k2, pass 2nd sl-st over the 2 knit sts, k1, sl 1, k2, psso the 2 knit sts; rep from *, end k1.

Row 10—With B, p2, * yo, p3, yo, p1, sl 1, p1; rep from *.

Row 11—With A, * k1, sl 1, k2, psso the 2 knit sts, sl 2, k2, pass 2nd sl-st over the 2 knit sts; rep from *, end k2.

Row 12—With A, * p3, yo, p1, sl 1, p1, yo; rep from *, end p2.

Row 13—With B, k4, * sl 1, k2, psso the 2 knit sts, sl 2, k2, pass 2nd sl-st over the 2 knit sts; k1; rep from *, end sl 1, k2, psso the 2 knit sts, sl 1, k2.

Row 14—With B, p2, * sl 1, p1, yo, p3, yo, p1; rep from *, end sl 1, p1, yo, p5.

Row 15—With A, k2, * sl 2, k2, pass 2nd sl-st over the 2 knit sts, k1, sl 1, k2, psso the 2 knit sts; rep from *.

Row 16—With A, * p1, yo, p3, yo, p1, sl 1; rep from *, end p2.

Repeat Rows 1-16.

Two-Color Dip Stitch

A dip stitch is made by the technique demonstrated here, of pulling a stitch through the fabric from several rows below. This pattern may be worked in solid color for an attractive texture; or, it may be shown on the wrong side. The rather unusual practice of showing "broken" color bands in the purl stitches gives this fabric a beaded effect.

Two-Color Dip Stitch

Multiple of 8 sts plus 3. Colors A and B.

Cast on with Color A and purl one row.

Rows 1 and 3 (Wrong side)—With B, purl.

Rows 2 and 4—With B, knit.

Row 5—With A, knit.

Row 6—With A, k1, * insert right-hand needle from front under purled loop of next st 6 rows below; knit an extra st in this st; then knit the next st on left-hand needle and pass the extra st over it (dip stitch made); k7; rep from *, end last repeat k1.

Rows 7 through 10—With B, repeat Rows 1 through 4.

Row 11—With A, knit.

Row 12—With A, k5, * make dip stitch as in Row 6, k7; rep from *, end last repeat k5.

Repeat Rows 1–12.

Dip-Stitch Check

Contributed by Toshiko Sugiyama, Oakland, California

Multiple of 4 sts plus 3. Colors A and B.

Rows 1 and 3 (Wrong side)—With A, purl.

Row 2—With A, knit.

Row 4—With B, k3, * insert needle into front of the 3rd st below the next st on left-hand needle, and draw up a loop; then knit the next st on left-hand needle and pass the loop over the st just knitted; k3; rep from *.

Rows 5, 6, and 7—With B, repeat Rows 1, 2, and 3.

Row 8—With A, k1, rep from * of Row 4; end last repeat k1 instead of k3.

Repeat Rows 1–8.

Dip-Stitch Check

Sunrise Shell Pattern *See color page xiii*

This striking three-color design bears some resemblance to a crocheted Shell Stitch, and makes beautiful handbags, cushions, afghans, hats, coats, and sweaters. Drop-stitches and *wrong*-side twists are used to make the pattern. The wrong-side Left Twist (LT) only sounds difficult; it is easy to work once the idea is grasped. Turning the work over slightly, so as to see the right side, insert the needle from the left into the back loop of the second stitch, then bring the needle point *around* the skipped stitch to the front, or wrong, side (where the yarn is held, waiting to purl); wrap yarn and purl, letting the needle point "back out" of the stitch in the usual way. Then work the skipped stitch as directed.

Multiple of 6 sts plus 3. Colors A, B, and C.

Cast on with Color A and purl one row.

NOTES: Right Twist (RT)—skip 1 st and purl the 2nd st, then purl the skipped st, then sl both sts from needle together.

Left Twist (LT)—skip 1 st and purl the 2nd st in *back* loop, then purl the skipped st in the usual way, then sl both sts from needle together.

PREPARATION ROWS

Rows 1 and 3 (Right side)—With B, knit.
Row 2—With B, purl.
Row 4—With B, p2, * RT, p1, LT, p1; rep from *, end p1.

End of preparation rows.

Row 5—With C, k4, * drop next st off needle and unravel 4 rows down; insert needle from front into the st in 5th row below and knit, catching the 4 loose strands in st; k5; rep from *, end last repeat k4.
Row 6—With C, purl.
Row 7—With C, knit.
Row 8—With C, p2, * LT, p1, RT, p1; rep from *, end p1.
Row 9—With A, k1, rep from * of Row 5; end last repeat k1 instead of k5.
Row 10—With A, purl.
Row 11—With A, knit.
Row 12—With A, p2, * RT, p1, LT, p1; rep from *, end p1.
Rows 13 through 16—With B, repeat Rows 5 through 8.
Rows 17 through 20—With C, repeat Rows 9 through 12.
Rows 21 through 24—With A, repeat Rows 5 through 8.
Rows 25 through 28—With B, repeat Rows 9 through 12.

Omitting preparation rows, repeat Rows 5–28.

English Rose Tweed *See color page xiv*

Here is a really lovely three-color pattern that is easy to work. It makes a flat, rather loose, and very wide fabric. Beware of casting on too many stitches, and be sure to bind off loosely.

This pattern will make charming sweaters, vests, jackets, coats, and children's wear. Try it in two or three different types of yarn—such as wool with ribbon, slubbed yarns with smooth, etc. The wrong side is beautiful, too.

Even number of sts. Colors A, B, and C.

Cast on with Color C and knit one row.

Row 1 (Right side)—With A, k1, * p1, k1 in the row below; rep from *, end k1.
Row 2—With A, knit.
Row 3—With B, k1, * k1 in the row below, p1; rep from *, end k1.
Row 4—With B, knit.
Rows 5 and 6—With C, repeat Rows 1 and 2.
Rows 7 and 8—With A, repeat Rows 3 and 4.
Rows 9 and 10—With B, repeat Rows 1 and 2.
Rows 11 and 12—With C, repeat Rows 3 and 4.

Repeat Rows 1–12.

Three-Color Daisy Stitch *See color page xiv*

Sometimes this pattern is referred to as Star Stitch—which is fair enough, as it does form little star-like motifs—but then it is often confused with the *other* Star Stitch which is worked in quite a different way. Daisy Stitch is beautiful in one, two, three or four colors; the three-color version here will suffice to demonstrate. Note that on the "p3 tog, yo, p3 tog again" operation, the stitches are *not* removed from the left-hand needle until the whole operation is completed.

Multiple of 4 sts plus 1. Colors A, B, and C.

Row 1 (Right side)—With A, knit.
Row 2—With A, k1, * p3 tog, yo, purl the same 3 sts tog again, k1; rep from *.
Row 3—With B, knit.
Row 4—With B, k1, p1, k1, * p3 tog, yo, purl the same 3 sts tog again, k1; rep from *, end p1, k1.
Rows 5 and 6—With C, repeat Rows 1 and 2.
Rows 7 and 8—With A, repeat Rows 3 and 4.
Rows 9 and 10—With B, repeat Rows 1 and 2.
Rows 11 and 12—With C, repeat Rows 3 and 4.

Repeat Rows 1–12.

Fan Dip Stitch

There are several details to be considered, if this pattern is to be worked most successfully. The "dipped" strands should not be twisted as they are passed over the subsequent stitch; therefore they must be turned *knitwise* as they are placed on the right-hand needle. To accomplish this, after drawing up the loop insert the left-hand needle behind the *back* strand of the loop, and through the loop to the front, slipping the loop onto the left-hand needle in this way. Then slip the loop *purlwise* back onto the right-hand needle, and it will be in the correct position. This "juggling" of the loop also affords an opportunity to lengthen it and loosen it; the pattern can be spoiled by work that is too tight. Notice that all three loops are taken from the *same* purled stitch 5 rows below.

This pattern need not be worked in two colors. It is an exceedingly pretty texture pattern when done in the same color throughout.

Multiple of 10 sts plus 2. Colors A and B.

Cast on with Color A and knit one row.

Row 1 (Wrong side)—With A, p8, * k1, p9; rep from *, end last repeat p3.

Rows 2 and 4—With B, knit.

Rows 3 and 5—With B, purl.

Row 6—With A, * (k1, insert right-hand needle from the front under the purled Color A st 5 rows below, and draw up a loop; knit next st and pass the loop over the st just worked) 3 times, k4; rep from *, end k2.

Row 7—With A, p3, * k1, p9; rep from *, end last repeat p8.

Rows 8, 9, 10, and 11—With B, repeat Rows 2, 3, 4, and 5.

Row 12—With A, k5, rep from * of Row 6: end last repeat k1 instead of k4.

Repeat Rows 1–12.

ABOVE: *Fan Dip Stitch*
BELOW: *Shell Dip Stitch*

Shell Dip Stitch

This pattern is similar in principle to Fan Dip Stitch, but the technique is a little different. The shells can be made by "dipping" the right-hand needle, but the use of a crochet hook gives more control of the length of the six loops, which should be reasonably uniform. To find the right stitch from which to take the loops, count 3 stitches over on the left-hand needle and then 3 ridges down, beginning with the ridge immediately under the needle. Insert hook under the third ridge, just above the last Color A row.

In a single color, Shell Dip Stitch is a very pretty texture pattern.

Multiple of 14 sts plus 2. Colors A and B.

Cast on with Color A and knit one row.

Rows 1, 2, 3, 4, 5, and 6—With B, knit.

Row 7 (Right side)—With A, k9, * (insert crochet hook into the front of st 5 rows below the 3rd st on left-hand needle, and draw through a long loop; sl this loop on right-hand needle, then knit the next st) 6 times, taking all 6 loops from the same st below; k8; rep from *, end last repeat k1.

Row 8—With A, k1, * (p2 tog-b) 3 times, p1, (p2 tog) 3 times, k7; rep from *, end k1.

Rows 9, 10, 11, 12, 13, and 14—With B, knit.

Row 15—With A, k2, rep from * of Row 7 across.

Row 16—With A, k8, * (p2 tog-b) 3 times, p1, (p2 tog) 3 times, k7; rep from *, end last repeat k1.

Repeat Rows 1–16.

Florentine Frieze

The elements of this pattern are simple—a few woven bands, a little quilting—but the finished effect is one of intricate and amazing beauty. The caught-up strands make shapes reminiscent of the famous "garland" frieze in baroque decoration. The pattern makes a stunning yoke for a Scandinavian-type sweater, or fancy mittens, or decorative bands around skirts and sleeves. It is very good also for home accessories such as cushions and slipcovers.

Multiple of 4 sts plus 1. Colors A and B.

Row 1 (Wrong side)—With A, purl.

Row 2—With B, k1, * sl 1 wyib, sl 1 wyif, sl 1 wyib, k1; rep from *.

Row 3—With B, p1, * sl 3 wyib, yo, p1; rep from *.

Row 4—With A, knit, dropping all yo's off needle to make long loose Color B strands across front of work.

Row 5—With A, purl.

Row 6—With B, k1, * sl 1 wyib, insert needle from front under the loose Color B strand and knit next st, bringing needle out under strand to catch strand behind st; sl 1 wyib, k1; rep from *.

Row 7—With B, k1, * sl 1 wyif, p1, sl 1 wyif, k1; rep from *.

Row 8—With A, knit.

Row 9—With A, purl.

Row 10—With B, k1, * sl 1 wyif, k1; rep from *.

Rows 11 through 20—Repeat Rows 1 through 10, reversing colors.

Repeat Rows 1–20.

Florentine Frieze

Bonbon Pattern *See color page xv*

Here is a pretty three-color pattern with one little twist stitch. If you do not know how to make a Left Twist (LT), see Glossary.

Multiple of 10 sts plus 4. Colors A, B, and C.

Row 1 (Wrong side)—With A, knit.
Row 2—With B, k6, * sl 2 wyib, k8; rep from *, end sl 2, k6.
Row 3—With B, p4, * sl 6 wyif, p4; rep from *.
Row 4—With B, k4, * sl 6 wyib, k4; rep from *.
Row 5—With B, p6, * sl 2 wyif, p8; rep from *, end sl 2, p6.
Row 6—With A, k6, * LT, k8; rep from *, end LT, k6.
Row 7—With A, knit.
Row 8—With C, k1, * sl 2 wyib, k8; rep from *, end sl 2, k1.
Row 9—With C, p1, sl 4 wyif, * p4, sl 6 wyif; rep from *, end p4, sl 4, p1.
Row 10—With C, k1, sl 4 wyib, * k4, sl 6 wyib; rep from *, end k4, sl 4, k1.
Row 11—With C, p1, * sl 2 wyif, p8; rep from *, end sl 2, p1.
Row 12—With A, k1, * LT, k8; rep from *, end LT, k1.

Repeat Rows 1–12.

Four-Color Blister Stitch *See color page xv*

This beautiful pattern is worked by the drop-stitch technique and is a 12-row repetition; the additional rows serve to alternate colors. The surface of the fabric is very "bumpy", each little blister standing out in relief against the Color A background.

Multiple of 4 sts plus 3. Colors A, B, C, and D.

Cast on with Color A and purl one row.

Rows 1 and 3 (Right side)—With B, knit.
Rows 2 and 4—With B, purl.
Row 5—With A, k3, * drop next st off needle and unravel 4 rows down; insert needle from front into Color A st in 5th row below and knit, catching the 4 loose strands in st; k3; rep from *.
Row 6—With A, purl.
Rows 7 through 10—With C, repeat Rows 1–4.
Row 11—With A, k1, rep from * of Row 5; end last repeat k1 instead of k3.
Row 12—With A, purl.

Rows 13 through 16—With D, repeat Rows 1-4.
Rows 17 and 18—With A, repeat Rows 5 and 6.
Rows 19 through 22—With B, repeat Rows 1-4.
Rows 23 and 24—With A, repeat Rows 11 and 12.
Rows 25 through 28—With C, repeat Rows 1-4.
Rows 29 and 30—With A, repeat Rows 5 and 6.
Rows 31 through 34—With D, repeat Rows 1-4.
Rows 35 and 36—With A, repeat Rows 11 and 12.

Repeat Rows 1–36.

Three Flowers *See color page xvi*

Here is a delightful pattern of knitted-in "embroidery", ideal for borders or accent bands (on a yoke, for instance). The pattern is shown in alternating bands of contrasting color, which is another pleasing idea for cushions, handbags, dirndls or Tyrolean vests. Multicolored odds and ends of yarn can be used up by making such articles in as many different-colored bands as desired.

Multiple of 10 sts plus 3. Colors A, B, and C.

Row 1 (Right side)—With A, knit.
Row 2—With A, purl.
Row 3—With B, knit.
Row 4—With B, k5, * k3 wrapping yarn 3 times for each st, k7; rep from *, end last repeat k5.
Row 5—With A, k1, * sl 1 wyib, k3, sl 3 wyib dropping extra wraps, k3; rep from *, end sl 1, k1.
Row 6—With A, p1, * sl 1 wyif, p3, sl 3 wyif, p3; rep from *, end sl 1, p1.
Row 7—With A, k5, * sl 3 wyib, k7; rep from *, end last repeat k5.
Row 8—With A, p5, * sl 3 wyif, p7; rep from *, end last repeat p5.
Row 9—With A, k3, * sl 2 wyib, drop next (1st Color B) st off needle to front of work, sl the same 2 sts back to left-hand needle, pick up dropped st and knit it; k3, drop next (3rd Color B) st off needle to front of work, k2, pick up dropped st and knit it; k3; rep from *.
Row 10—With C, p1, sl 2 wyif, * [(p1, k1, p1) in next st, sl 2 wyif] twice, (p1, k1, p1) in next st, sl 3 wyif; rep from *, end [(p1, k1, p1) in next st, sl 2 wyif] 3 times, p1.
Row 11—With C, k1, sl 2 wyib, * Make Bobble (MB) in next 3 (increased) sts as follows: p3, turn and k3, turn and sl 1—k2 tog—psso, completing bobble; (sl 2 wyib, MB) twice, sl 3 wyib; rep from *, end (MB, sl 2 wyib) 3 times, k1.
Row 12—With A, purl, purling into the *back* of each bobble st.
Rows 13 and 14—With A, repeat Rows 1 and 2.

Repeat Rows 1–14.

NOTE: Garter-stitch stripes of different colors may be inserted between repeats.

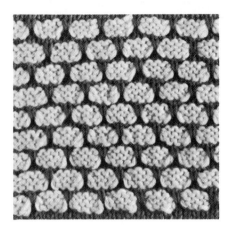

Paving Stones

Paving Stones

Contributed by Hildegard M. Elsner, Aldan, Pennsylvania

Here is a drop-stitch pattern with purled rows on the right side, giving an impression of rough-hewn rectangular blocks set in a wall or pavement. The wrong side of the fabric is attractive, showing deeply indented Color B knit stitches outlined by purl in the manner of the Two-Color Dip Stitch. (See also Four-Color Blister Stitch.)

Multiple of 4 sts plus 1. Colors A and B.

Cast on with Color A and knit one row.

Row 1 (Wrong side)—With A, purl.
Rows 2 and 3—With B, knit.
Row 4—With B, purl.
Row 5—With B, knit.
Row 6—With A, k2, * drop next st off needle and unravel 4 rows down; insert needle into the front of Color A st in 5th row below and knit, catching the 4 loose strands in st; k3; rep from *, end last repeat k2.
Rows 7, 8, 9, 10, and 11—Repeat Rows 1, 2, 3, 4, and 5.
Row 12—With A, k4, rep from * of Row 6; end k1.

Repeat Rows 1–12.

Knitter's Choice
ABOVE: *First decrease*
CENTER: *Second decrease*
BELOW: *Third decrease*

Knitter's Choice

Choose one of three different types of decrease, here, to make the puffy Color B motifs the shape that you prefer. The first decrease, a simple k5 tog-b, swirls the long stitches to the left. The second makes a square shape with Color A stitches encroaching at the top. The third makes the central stitch prominent. Another idea is to work the pattern in more than two colors, using a different decrease in each different-colored row of puffs.

Multiple of 4 sts plus 1. Colors A and B.

Cast on with Color A and knit two rows.

NOTES: First decrease—k5 tog-b.
Second decrease—k2 tog-b, k3 tog, then pass the k2-tog-b st over the k3-tog st.
Third decrease—insert needle into first 3 sts as if to k3 tog, and *slip* the sts from this position; k2 tog, then pass the 3 slipped sts all together over the k2-tog st.

Row 1 (Right side)—With B, k2, * sl 1 wyib, k1, (k1, yo, k1, yo, k1) in next st, k1; rep from *, end sl 1 wyib, k2.

Row 2—With B, k2, * sl 1 wyif, k1, k5 wrapping yarn twice for each st, k1; rep from *, end sl 1 wyif, k2.

Row 3—With A, k4, * sl 5 wyib dropping extra wraps, k3; rep from *, end k1.

Rows 4 and 6—With A, k4, * sl 5 wyif, k3; rep from *, end k1.

Row 5—With A, k4, * sl 5 wyib, k3; rep from *, end k1.

Row 7—With A, k4, * work next 5 sts tog using first, second, or third decrease, k3; rep from *, end k1.

Row 8—With A, knit.

Row 9—With B, k2, * (k1, yo, k1, yo, k1) in next st, k1, sl 1 wyib, k1; rep from *, end (k1, yo, k1, yo, k1) in next st, k2.

Row 10—With B, k2, * k5 wrapping yarn twice for each st, k1, sl 1 wyif, k1; rep from *, end k5 wrapping yarn twice for each st, k2.

Row 11—With A, k2, * sl 5 wyib dropping extra wraps, k3; rep from *, end last repeat k2.

Rows 12 and 14—With A, k2, * sl 5 wyif, k3; rep from *, end last repeat k2.

Row 13—With A, k2, * sl 5 wyib, k3; rep from *, end last repeat k2.

Row 15—With A, k2, * work next 5 sts tog using first, second, or third decrease, k3; rep from *, end last repeat k2.

Row 16—With A, knit.

Repeat Rows 1–16.

Crazy Quilted Pattern

This pattern is done in two colors for greater contrast. The passing of the yo's over subsequent stitches is delayed 4 rows, so that the yo's are elongated into V-shaped quilting strands. The result is a novelty fabric with isolated openings and considerable texture interest.

Multiple of 3 sts plus 2. Colors A and B.

Cast on with A and knit one row.

Row 1 (Wrong side)—With A, k1, * p3, (yo) twice; rep from *, end k1.

Row 2—With B, k1, * sl the yo st wyib, dropping 2nd yo off needle; k3; rep from *, end k1.

Rows 3 and 5—With B, k1, * p3, sl 1 wyif; rep from *, end k1.

Row 4—With B, k1, * sl 1 wyib, k3; rep from *, end k1.

Row 6—With A, k1, * sl 1 wyib (this is the Color A yo st), k3, psso the 3 knit sts; rep from *, end k1.

Repeat Rows 1–6.

Crazy Quilted Pattern

Long Bobble Pattern

These bold pear-shaped bobbles are ingeniously constructed of a central increase, four turning rows, and two lateral decreases on the return row; then the entire assemblage is carried upward for 5 rows more by slipping the stitches. Packing these unusual bobbles close together, this pattern makes a very thick novelty fabric for hats, cushions, handbags, patch pockets, afghan squares, borders, etc. After having learned how to make this type of bobble, the knitter may use it also in other contexts.

Multiple of 6 sts plus 3. (15 sts minimum) Colors A and B.

Cast on with Color A and knit one row.

Row 1 (Right side)—With B, k1, * sl 1 wyib, k2, (k1, yo, k1) in next st, k1, (turn and p5, turn and k5) twice, k1; rep from *, end sl 1 wyib, k1.

Row 2—With B, k1, * sl 1 wyif, k1, p2 tog, p1, p2 tog-b, k1; rep from *, end sl 1 wyif, k1.

Rows 3, 5, and 7—With A, k3, * sl 3 wyib, k3; rep from *.

Rows 4 and 6—With A, k3, * sl 3 wyif, k3; rep from *.

Row 8—With A, k3, * p3, k3; rep from *.

Row 9—With B, k4, rep from * of Row 1: end sl 1 wyib, k4.

Row 10—With B, k4, rep from * of Row 2; end sl 1 wyif, k4.

Rows 11, 13, and 15—With A, k6, * sl 3 wyib, k3; rep from *, end k3.

Rows 12 and 14—With A, k6, * sl 3 wyif, k3; rep from *, end k3.

Row 16—With A, k6, * p3, k3; rep from *, end k3.

Repeat Rows 1–16.

Long Bobble Pattern

Puffball Plaid

Puffball Plaid

A puffball is like a bobble—a knobby, knot-like formation made in a single stitch—but notice the difference here in the manner of working it. Each new loop is placed on the left-hand needle and then knitted, exactly as in the method of casting on that is called "knitting-on". Puffballs can also be used as spot-patterns on a plain solid-color stockinette fabric, or to replace bobbles or popcorns in any fancy pattern.

Multiple of 9 sts plus 4. Colors A and B.

Row 1 (Wrong side)—With A, purl.
Row 2—With A, knit.
Row 3—With A, k1, * p2, k7; rep from *, end p2, k1.

Row 4—With A, k1, * k2 wrapping yarn twice for each st, k7; rep from *, end k2 wrapping yarn twice, k1.

Row 5—With B, k1, * sl 2 wyif dropping extra wraps, p7; rep from *, end sl 2, k1.

Row 6—With B, k1, * sl 2 wyib, k7; rep from *, end sl 2, k1.

Row 7—With B, k1, * sl 2 wyif, p7; rep from *, end sl 2, k1.

Row 8—Repeat Row 6.

Row 9—With A, k1, * p2, sl 3 wyif, p1, sl 3 wyif; rep from *, end p2, k1.

Row 10—With A, k1, * k2 wrapping yarn twice for each st, sl 3 wyib, make Puffball in next st as follows: insert needle in st as if to knit, draw through a loop and place this loop on left-hand needle; (insert needle into front of new loop and knit, then place next new loop on left-hand needle) 4 times, making 5 new loops in all; then k6 (the 5 new loops, plus the original st); then pass the 2nd, 3rd, 4th, 5th and 6th sts on right-hand needle one at a time over the 1st (original) st, completing Puffball; sl 3 wyib; rep from *, end k2 wrapping yarn twice, k1.

Rows 11 and 12—With B, repeat Rows 5 and 6.

Repeat Rows 1–12.

Cluster Quilting

This beautiful pattern is made by a fascinatingly unusual technique that is much less complicated than it seems at first glance. Novice knitters are likely to be frightened by the long lines of loose stitches dropped off the needle in Rows 4 and 10, looking as though they might disappear forever. But don't worry—they won't. The following rows pick them up again very neatly, one at a time. Since the dropped stitches are never crossed, there is no problem about knowing which one to pick up next; it is always the nearest one available.

Multiple of 8 sts plus 1. Colors A and B.

Preparation row, wrong side—With A, p1, * p1 wrapping yarn twice, p5, p1 wrapping yarn twice, p1; rep from *.

Row 1—With B, k1, * sl 1 wyib dropping extra wrap, k5, sl 1 wyib dropping extra wrap, k1; rep from *.

Row 2—With B, p1, * sl 1 wyif, p5, sl 1 wyif, p1; rep from *.

Row 3—With B, k1, * sl 1 wyib, k5, sl 1 wyib, k1; rep from *.

Cluster Quilting

Row 4—With B, purl, dropping all elongated Color A sl-sts off needle to back (i.e., to *right* side of fabric).

Row 5—With A, k1, sl 1 wyib, k1, * pick up first dropped st and knit it, k1, pick up next dropped st and knit it; then (with yarn in back sl the last 3 sts worked back to left-hand needle, pass yarn to front, sl the same 3 sts back again to right-hand needle, pass yarn to back) twice; k1, sl 3 wyib, k1; rep from *, end last repeat sl 1 wyib, k1 instead of sl 3 wyib, k1.

Row 6—With A, p1, sl 1 wyif, * (p1, p1 wrapping yarn twice) twice, p1, sl 3 wyif; rep from *, end last repeat sl 1 wyif, p1 instead of sl 3 wyif.

Row 7—With B, k3, * sl 1 wyib dropping extra wrap, k1, sl 1 wyib dropping extra wrap, k5; rep from *, end last repeat k3.

Row 8—With B, p3, * sl 1 wyif, p1, sl 1 wyif, p5; rep from *, end last repeat p3.

Row 9—With B, k3, * sl 1 wyib, k1, sl 1 wyib, k5; rep from *, end last repeat k3.

Row 10—With B, purl, dropping all elongated Color A sl-sts off needle to back.

Row 11—With A, k1, pick up first dropped st and knit it, k1, sl 3 wyib, k1; rep from * of Row 5; end pick up last dropped st and knit it, k1.

Row 12—With A, p1, * p1 wrapping yarn twice, p1, sl 3 wyif, p1, p1 wrapping yarn twice, p1; rep from *.

Omitting preparation row, repeat Rows 1–12.

Snowball Stitch

Snowball Stitch

Here is an unusual color-and-texture pattern with large purled clusters showing through a fabric of crossed elongated stitches. The effect is gay and informal, and the knitting firm and dense; so this pattern is ideal for warm ski sweaters, hats, and children's sportswear. It will also make cheerful cushion covers, extra-fancy sock tops, afghan squares, patch pockets and collars.

Multiple of 5 sts plus 1. Colors A and B.

Row 1 (Wrong side)—With A, purl.

Row 2—With A, knit.

Row 3—With A, p1, * p1 wrapping yarn twice around needle, p2, p1 wrapping yarn twice, p1; rep from *.

Row 4—With B, k1, * sl 1 wyib dropping extra wrap, k2, sl 1 wyib dropping extra wrap, (k1, yo, k1, yo, k1) in next st; rep from * across to last st, end last repeat with a plain k1.

Row 5—With B, k1, * sl 1 wyif, p2, sl 1 wyif, k5; rep from *, end sl 1, p2, sl 1, k1.

Row 6—With B, k1, * sl 1 wyib, k2, sl 1 wyib, p5; rep from *, end sl 1, k2, sl 1, k1.

Row 7—With B, k1, * sl 1 wyif, p2, sl 1 wyif, k2 tog, k3 tog, pass the k2-tog st over the k3-tog st; rep from *, end sl 1, p2, sl 1, k1.

Row 8—With A, k1, * drop first elongated st off needle to front of work, sl 2 wyib, drop next elongated st off needle to front; with left-hand needle pick up the first elongated st, sl the same 2 sts back to left-hand needle, then pick up the second elongated st onto left-hand needle, k5; rep from *.

Repeat Rows 1–8.

Picot Stripe

These decorative stripes have a lot of texture interest. The cleverly-constructed picot points are nubby, and stand out somewhat from the background. This pattern makes excellent borders for collars, cuffs, and pockets, and is very attractive in ski sweaters.

Multiple of 10 sts. Colors A and B.

Row 1 (Wrong side)—With A, purl.

Row 2—With B, k2, * (k1, yo, k1, yo, k1, yo, k1) in next st, making seven sts from one; k9; rep from *, end last repeat k7.

Row 3—With B, knit.

Row 4—With A, k1, * k2 tog, k5, ssk, k7; rep from *, end last repeat k6.

Row 5—With A, p6, * p2 tog-b, p1, sl 1 wyif, p1, p2 tog, p7; rep from *, end last repeat p1.

Row 6—With A, k1, * k2 tog, sl 1 wyib, ssk, k7; rep from *, end last repeat k6.

Row 7—With A, purl.

Row 8—With B, k7, * (k1, yo, k1, yo, k1, yo, k1) in next st, k9; rep from *, end last repeat k2.

Row 9—With B, knit.

Row 10—With A, k6, * k2 tog, k5, ssk, k7; rep from *, end last repeat k1.

Row 11—With A, p1, * p2 tog-b, p1, sl 1 wyif, p1, p2 tog, p7; rep from *, end last repeat p6.

Row 12—With A, k6, * k2 tog, sl 1 wyib, ssk, k7; rep from *, end last repeat k1.

Repeat Rows 1–12.

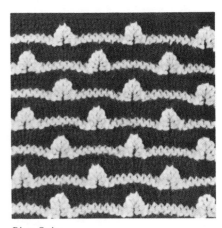

Picot Stripe

Swallowtail Quilting

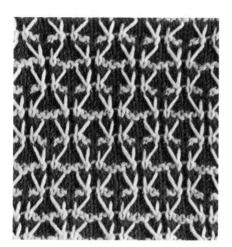

Swallowtail Quilting

This fancy design is an amalgam of three patterns. First, there is the simple stripe pattern of Rows 1–6; then there are two different half-drop patterns, one contained by Rows 1–6, 19–23, and 18; the other by Rows 13–17, 24 and 25, 2–5, and 12. Note that in these composite directions Row 1 does not appear again as Row 1 (it is replaced by Row 25), but it does reappear as Row 7.

"Knit the sl-st over" and "knit through the sl-st" are two actions with which the knitter may be unfamiliar, though they are not difficult to perform. To knit the sl-st over, pass the needle-point in front of the required number of skipped stitches (in this case, two), insert it into the front loop of the sl-st, then pass the needle-point back again in front of the same skipped stitches, catch the yarn to the right of the first stitch and knit, taking the sl-st off the left-hand needle but being careful not to let the two skipped stitches come off with it. To knit through the sl-st, insert the needle-point purlwise into the sl-st as if to slip it again, but do not slip it; knit the first stitch beyond it and bring this stitch back through the sl-st and off the left-hand needle, being careful not to let the sl-st come off too. This action can be repeated as many times as necessary—twice, in this pattern.

Multiple of 8 sts plus 1. Colors A and B.

Row 1 (Preparation—wrong side)—With A, k3, * p1, k1, p1, k5; rep from *, end last repeat k3.

Rows 2 and 4—With B, k3, * sl 1 wyib, k1, sl 1 wyib, k5; rep from *, end last repeat k3.

Rows 3 and 5—With B, p3, * sl 1 wyif, p1, sl 1 wyif, p5; rep from *, end last repeat p3.

Row 6—With A, k1, * skip 2 sts, knit Color A sl-st over the 2 skipped sts; k3, skip next Color A sl-st, knit next 2 sts through the sl-st, then knit the sl-st in back loop; k1; rep from *.

Rows 7 through 11—Repeat Rows 1 through 5.

Row 12—With A, k1, * skip 2 sts, knit Color A sl-st over the 2 skipped sts, k2, sl 1 wyib, skip next Color A sl-st, knit next 2 sts through the sl-st, then knit the sl-st in back loop; k1; rep from *.

Row 13—With A, k1, * p1, k2, sl 1 wyif, k2, p1, k1; rep from *.

Rows 14 and 16—With B, k1, * sl 1 wyib, k5, sl 1 wyib, k1; rep from *.

Rows 15 and 17—With B, p1, * sl 1 wyif, p5, sl 1 wyif, p1; rep from *.

Row 18—With A, k1, * skip Color A sl-st, knit next 2 sts through the sl-st, then knit the sl-st in back loop; k1, skip next 2 sts, knit next Color A sl-st over the 2 skipped sts, k3; rep from *.

Row 19—With A, k1, * p1, k5, p1, k1; rep from *.

Rows 20 through 23—Repeat Rows 14 through 17.

Row 24—With A, k1, * skip Color A sl-st, knit next 2 sts through the sl-st, then knit the sl-st in back loop; k1, skip next 2 sts, knit next Color A sl-st over the 2 skipped sts; k2, sl 1 wyib; rep from *, end last repeat k1 instead of sl 1.

Row 25—With A, k3, * p1, k1, p1, k2, sl 1 wyif, k2; rep from *, end p1, k1, p1, k3.

Omitting preparation row, repeat Rows 2–25.

House of Cards

Here is a fascinating pattern incorporating yarn-over stitches, slip-stitches, and contrasting colors. The stitch count varies; on Rows 2, 8, 14, and 20 the yarn-overs form increases; on Rows 6, 12, 18, and 24 the corresponding decreases are made to restore the original number of stitches. Each of these decreases includes a Color A slip-stitch carried from four rows below, and the Color B stitch adjoining it.

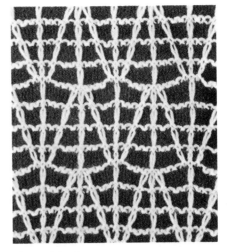

House of Cards

Multiple of 12 sts plus 3. Colors A and B.

NOTE: On right-side (even-numbered) rows, sl all sl-sts with yarn in back; on wrong-side (odd-numbered) rows, sl all sl-sts with yarn in front.

Row 1 (Wrong side)—With A, knit.
Row 2—With B, k1, * sl 1, k4, (sl 1, yo) twice, sl 1, k4; rep from *, end sl 1, k1. (On this row care must be taken to keep the 2 yo's strictly positioned between the 3 sl-sts. The central arrangement will be a double yo in Color B sts divided by a slipped Color A st.)
Row 3—With B, k1, * sl 1, p4, sl 1, purl the 1st yo, sl 1, knit the next yo, sl 1, p4; rep from *, end sl 1, k1. (On this row the same yo sts and sl-sts must be kept in strict order. Be sure the 1st Color A sl-st of the group is slipped onto right-hand needle *before* the following yo is worked. The same caution will apply to Rows 9, 15, and 21.)
Row 4—With B, k1, * sl 1, k4, (sl 1, k1) twice, sl 1, k4; rep from *, end sl 1, k1.
Row 5—With B, k1, * sl 1, p4, (sl 1, p1) twice, sl 1, p4; rep from *, end sl 1, k1.
Row 6—With A, k5, * k2 tog, k3, ssk, k7; rep from *, end last repeat k5.
Row 7—With A, knit.
Row 8—With B, k1, * sl 1, k3, sl 1, yo, k1, sl 1, k1, yo, sl 1, k3; rep from *, end sl 1, k1.

Row 9—With B, k1, * sl 1, p3, sl 1, p2, sl 1, p2, sl 1, p3; rep from *, end sl 1, k1.
Row 10—With B, k1, * sl 1, k3, sl 1, k2, sl 1, k2, sl 1, k3; rep from *, end sl 1, k1.
Row 11—With B, repeat Row 9.
Row 12—With A, k4, * k2 tog, k5, ssk, k5; rep from *, end last repeat k4.
Row 13—With A, knit.
Row 14—With B, k1, * sl 1, k2, sl 1, yo, k2, sl 1, k2, yo, sl 1, k2; rep from *, end sl 1, k1.
Row 15—With B, k1, * sl 1, p2, (sl 1, p3) twice, sl 1, p2; rep from *, end sl 1, k1.
Row 16—With B, k1, * sl 1, k2, (sl 1, k3) twice, sl 1, k2; rep from *, end sl 1, k1.
Row 17—With B, repeat Row 15.
Row 18—With A, k3, * k2 tog, k7, ssk, k3; rep from *.
Row 19—With A, knit.
Row 20—With B, k1, * sl 1, k1, sl 1, yo, k3, sl 1, k3, yo, sl 1, k1; rep from *, end sl 1, k1.
Row 21—With B, k1, * sl 1, p1, (sl 1, p4) twice, sl 1, p1; rep from *, end sl 1, k1.
Row 22—With B, k1, * sl 1, k1, (sl 1, k4) twice, sl 1, k1; rep from *, end sl 1, k1.
Row 23—With B, repeat Row 21.
Row 24—With A, k2, * k2 tog, k9, ssk, k1; rep from *, end k1.

Repeat Rows 1–24.

Maltese Cross

In this pattern a slight variation on Three-and-One Tweed makes a surprisingly large difference.

Multiple of 4 sts plus 3. Colors A and B.

Row 1 (Wrong side)—With A, purl.
Row 2—With B, k3, * sl 1 wyib, k3; rep from *.
Row 3—With B, k3, * sl 1 wyif, k3; rep from *.
Row 4—With A, k1, * sl 1 wyib, k3; rep from *, end sl 1, k1.
Row 5—With A, k1, * sl 1 wyif, k3; rep from *, end sl 1, k1.
Row 6—With B, repeat Row 2.
Row 7—With B, purl.
Row 8—With A, repeat Row 4.

Maltese Cross

Repeat Rows 1–8.

Mosaic Patterns

Mosaic patterns are sophisticated designs in slip-stitch color knitting. The patterns themselves are complicated, but the knitting technique is not. Here, the most straight-forward principle of slip-stitch color knitting is applied to a number of complex geometrical shapes, illustrating the enormous variety and flexibility of one simple knitting method. The basic principle is this: portions of each row are hidden behind slipped stitches carried up from a different-colored row below. This means that (1) every slip-stitch is slipped with yarn in *back* on right-side rows, and the same stitch is slipped again, but with yarn in *front,* on wrong-side rows. (2) Colors are alternated every two rows, and (3) each slip-stitch spans two rows and is caught again with its own color on the third row.

Most of these patterns call for *knitting* wrong-side rows, which gives the fabric a nubby garter-stitch texture. But *purling* can be substituted at will, if a smooth stock-inette-type texture is desired. Some patterns look better one way, some the other; it depends upon the taste of the individual knitter, and upon the individual way of knitting. Remember, though, that if a pattern is shown in garter stitch, a stockinette version of the same pattern will look slightly elongated vertically. Conversely, a stockinette-type pattern will broaden and shorten a little when worked in garter stitch.

There is, then, nothing special about the method of making mosaics. It is a way of using colors which precludes having to change yarns in mid-row and strand across the back, as in "Fair Isle" knitting. Thus there are no bobbins, and no thickening of the fabric due to unused strands lying on the back. The method is superior to "Fair Isle" knitting except for one limitation: each area of "solid" color must contain dots of the opposite color. The reason for this is that the yarn must be caught and knitted at least every third stitch, lest the intervening slip-stitches be unattractively squeezed together.

Although the knitting technique is simple and easy, the pattern directions, in most cases, tend to be long. Therefore they must be read carefully as the work progresses. This diversity of rows, however, produces fanciful and charming designs with an intricate interplay of color. The variety of designs that can be made in this way is incredible; it is literally endless.

Now here is the most fascinating fact about mosaic patterns in general: *they can be worked on any number of stitches at all!* There is no need for the knitter to figure the closest multiple for a given size, or to juggle the pattern so as to work half a repeat or a third of a repeat for the sake of an extra inch. All that is necessary is to cast on the number of stitches that you want, then begin each pattern row at the right-hand edge according to the directions, and work across until you run out of stitches. If the row comes to an end in the middle of a repeat, it makes no difference! The return row is worked by knitting (or purling) and slipping the same stitches that were worked on the preceding row—so the beginning of the wrong-side row is not critical, and there are no special directions for it. All you have to do is look at the work to see which stitches were used in the preceding row, and which were not. You can "center" the pattern by using the recommended multiple of stitches if it is possible. But if, for reasons of size, this is not possible—you can forget it!

The patterns given here do not represent a really thorough exploration of all possible designs in mosaic knitting. On the contrary, they are just a beginning. Once the easy technique of mosaic knitting is clearly understood, any number of new and original patterns can be devised. In knitting as in most other creative crafts, simplicity means versatility. Mosaic knitting features a technique of the utmost simplicity and an application as broad as human ingenuity itself.

Two "Beginner's Mosaics"— Macedonian Stitch and Russian Stitch

I. MACEDONIAN STITCH

Multiple of 4 sts plus 3. Colors A and B.

Row 1 (Right side)—With A, knit.
Row 2—With A, purl.
Row 3—With B, k3, * sl 1 wyib, k3; rep from *.
Row 4—With B, k3, * sl 1 wyif, k3; rep from *.
Row 5—With A, k2, * sl 1 wyib, k1; rep from *, end k1.
Row 6—With A, p2, * sl 1 wyif, p1; rep from *, end p1.
Row 7—With B, k1, * sl 1 wyib, k3; rep from *, end sl 1, k1.
Row 8—With B, k1, * sl 1 wyif, k3; rep from *, end sl 1, k1.
Rows 9 and 10—With A, repeat Rows 1 and 2.
Rows 11 and 12—With B, repeat Rows 7 and 8.
Rows 13 and 14—With A, repeat Rows 5 and 6.
Rows 15 and 16—With B, repeat Rows 3 and 4.

Repeat Rows 1–16.

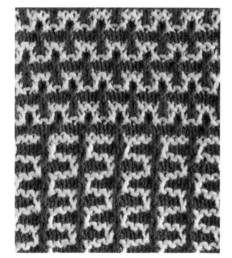

ABOVE: *Macedonian Stitch*
BELOW: *Russian Stitch*

II. RUSSIAN STITCH

Multiple of 5 sts plus 1. Colors A and B.

Cast on with Color A and knit one row.

Row 1 (Right side)—With B, * k4, sl 1 wyib; rep from *, end k1.

Row 2—With B, p1, * sl 1 wyif, p4; rep from *.

Row 3—With A, k5, * sl 1 wyib, k4; rep from *, end k1.

Row 4—With A, k5, * sl 1 wyif, k4; rep from *, end k1.

Row 5—With B, k1, * sl 1 wyib, k4; rep from *.

Row 6—With B, * p4, sl 1 wyif; rep from *, end p1.

Rows 7 and 8—With A, repeat Rows 3 and 4.

Repeat Rows 1–8.

Sliding Bricks

Multiple of 15 sts plus 2. Colors A and B.

Cast on with Color A and purl one row.

NOTE: On all right-side (odd-numbered) rows, sl all sl-sts with yarn in *back*. All wrong-side rows use the same color as the preceding right-side row.

Row 1 (Right side)—With B, k1, * (k1, sl 1) twice, k10, sl 1; rep from *, end k1.

Row 2 and all other wrong-side rows using Color B—*Knit* all sts knitted on previous row; sl all the same sl-sts with yarn in *front*.

Row 3—With A, k5, * sl 1, k4, sl 1, k9; rep from *, end last repeat k6.

Row 4 and all other wrong-side rows using Color A—*Purl* all sts knitted on previous row; sl all the same sl-sts with yarn in *front*.

Row 5—With B, k1, * k10, (sl 1, k1) twice, sl 1; rep from *, end k1.

Row 7—With A, k1, * sl 1, k4, sl 1, k9; rep from *, end k1.

Row 9—With B, k7, * (sl 1, k1) twice, sl 1, k10; rep from *, end last repeat k5.

Row 11—With A, k2, * sl 1, k9, sl 1, k4; rep from *.

Rows 13 and 14—With B, repeat Rows 9 and 10.

Rows 15 and 16—With A, repeat Rows 7 and 8.

Rows 17 and 18—With B, repeat Rows 5 and 6.

Rows 19 and 20—With A, repeat Rows 3 and 4.

Rows 21 and 22—With B, repeat Rows 1 and 2.

Row 23—With A, * k9, sl 1, k4, sl 1; rep from *, end k2.

Row 24—See Row 4.

Repeat Rows 1–24.

Sliding Bricks

Three-and-One Mosaic

Three-and-One Mosaic

Multiple of 4 sts plus 3. Colors A and B.

Row 1 (Right side)—With A, knit.
Row 2—With A, knit.
Row 3—With B, k3, * sl 1 wyib, k3; rep from *.
Row 4—With B, k3, * sl 1 wyif, k3; rep from *.
Row 5—With A, k1, * sl 1 wyib, k3; rep from *, end sl 1, k1.
Row 6—With A, k1, * sl 1 wyif, k3; rep from *, end sl 1, k1.
Row 7—With B, k2, * sl 1 wyib, k1; rep from *, end k1.
Row 8—With B, k2, * sl 1 wyif, k1; rep from *, end k1.
Rows 9 and 10—With A, repeat Rows 3 and 4.
Rows 11 and 12—With B, repeat Rows 5 and 6.
Rows 13 and 14—With A, knit.
Rows 15 and 16—Repeat Rows 11 and 12.
Rows 17 and 18—Repeat Rows 9 and 10.
Rows 19 and 20—Repeat Rows 7 and 8.
Rows 21 and 22—Repeat Rows 5 and 6.
Rows 23 and 24—Repeat Rows 3 and 4.

Repeat Rows 1–24.

Chessboard

Chessboard

Multiple of 14 sts plus 2. Colors A and B.

NOTE: On all right-side rows, sl all sl-sts with yarn in *back*.

Rows 1 and 2—With A, knit.
Rows 3, 7, 11, and 15 (Right side)—With B, k1, * k7, (sl 1, k1) 3 times, sl 1; rep from *, end k1.
Row 4 and all other wrong-side rows—Knit the same sts worked on previous row, with the same color; sl all the same sl-sts with yarn in *front*.
Rows 5, 9, and 13—With A, k1, * (sl 1, k1) 3 times, sl 1, k7; rep from *, end k1.
Rows 17 and 18—With A, knit.
Rows 19, 23, 27, and 31—With B, k1, * (sl 1, k1) 3 times, sl 1, k7; rep from *, end k1.
Rows 21, 25, and 29—With A, k1, * k7, (sl 1, k1) 3 times, sl 1; rep from *, end k1.
Row 32—See Row 4.

Repeat Rows 1–32.

Wave

Multiple of 5 sts plus 2. Colors A and B.

Cast on with A and knit one row.

NOTE: On all right-side rows sl all sl-sts with yarn in *back*.

Row 1 (Right side)—With B, k5, * sl 1, k4; rep from *, end sl 1, k1.

Row 2 and all other wrong-side rows—Knit (or purl) the same sts worked on previous row, with the same color; sl all the same sl-sts with yarn in *front*.

Row 3—With A, k1, * sl 1, k4; rep from *, end k1.

Row 5—With B, k2, * sl 1, k4; rep from *.

Row 7—With A, k3, * sl 1, k4; rep from *, end sl 1, k3.

Row 9—With B, * k4, sl 1; rep from *, end k2.

Row 11—With A, repeat Row 1.

Row 13—With B, repeat Row 3.

Row 15—With A, repeat Row 5.

Row 17—With B, repeat Row 7.

Rows 19, 21, 23, 25, 27, 29, and 31—Repeat Rows 15, 13, 11, 9, 7, 5, and 3.

Row 32—See Row 2.

Repeat Rows 1–32.

LEFT: *Wave*
RIGHT: *Dotted Wave*

Dotted Wave

Multiple of 6 sts plus 2. Colors A and B.

Cast on with B and knit one row.

NOTE: On all right-side rows, sl all sl-sts with yarn in *back*.

Row 1 (Right side)—With A, * k5, sl 1; rep from *, end k2.

Row 2 and all other wrong-side rows—Knit (or purl) the same sts worked on previous row, with the same color; sl all the same sl-sts with yarn in *front*.

Row 3—With B, k2, * sl 1, k3, sl 1, k1; rep from *.

Row 5—With A, k3, * sl 1, k5; rep from *, end sl 1, k4.

Row 7—With B, k4, * sl 1, k1, sl 1, k3; rep from *, end (sl 1, k1) twice.

Row 9—With A, k1, * sl 1, k5; rep from *, end k1.

Row 11—With B, k2, * sl 1, k1, sl 1, k3; rep from *.

Rows 13, 15, 17, 19, and 21—Repeat Rows 1, 3, 5, 7, and 9.

Rows 23, 25, 27, and 29—Repeat Rows 7, 5, 3, and 1.

Rows 31, 33, 35, 37, and 39—Repeat Rows 11, 9, 7, 5, and 3.

Row 40—See Row 2.

Repeat Rows 1–40.

ABOVE: *Little Castle*
BELOW, LEFT: *Sliding Block Pattern*
BELOW, RIGHT: *Cage Pattern*

Three Reversible-Texture Mosaics: Little Castle, Sliding Block Pattern, and Cage Pattern

All three of these patterns combine knit and purl stitches on the wrong-side rows to make varying texture effects. These effects can be reversed, by reading "knit" for "purl" and vice versa *on the wrong-side* rows only. Or, a straight stockinette or garter-stitch type of fabric can be achieved by purling all the wrong-side stitches, in the first case, or knitting them, in the second.

I. LITTLE CASTLE

Multiple of 8 sts plus 5. Colors A and B.

Cast on with Color A and purl one row.

Row 1 (Right side)—With B, k4, * sl 1 wyib, k3; rep from *, end k1.
Row 2—With B, k4, * sl 1 wyif, k3; rep from *, end k1.
Row 3—With A, k1, * sl 1 wyib, k1; rep from *.
Row 4—With A, p1, * sl 1 wyif, k1, sl 1 wyif, p1; rep from *.
Row 5—With B, k2, * sl 1 wyib, k7; rep from *, end sl 1, k2.
Row 6—With B, k2, * sl 1 wyif, k7; rep from *, end sl 1, k2.
Row 7—With A, k1, * sl 1 wyib, k1, sl 1 wyib, k5; rep from *, end last repeat k1.
Row 8—With A, p1, * sl 1 wyif, k1, sl 1 wyif, p5; rep from *, end last repeat p1.
Rows 9, 10, 11, and 12—Repeat Rows 1, 2, 3, and 4.
Row 13—With B, k6, * sl 1 wyib, k7; rep from *, end last repeat k6.
Row 14—With B, k6, * sl 1 wyif, k7; rep from *, end last repeat k6.
Row 15—With A, k5, * sl 1 wyib, k1, sl 1 wyib, k5; rep from *.
Row 16—With A, p5, * sl 1 wyif, k1, sl 1 wyif, p5; rep from *.

Repeat Rows 1–16.

II. SLIDING BLOCK PATTERN

Multiple of 6 sts plus 3. Colors A and B.

Cast on with Color A and knit one row.

Row 1 (Right side)—With B, * k5, sl 1 wyib; rep from *, end k3.
Row 2—With B, p3, * sl 1 wyif, p5; rep from *.
Row 3—With A, k1, * sl 1 wyib, k5; rep from *, end sl 1, k1.
Row 4—With A, k1, * sl 1 wyif, k5; rep from *, end sl 1, k1.
Row 5—With B, k3, * sl 1 wyib, k5; rep from *.
Row 6—With B, * p5, sl 1 wyif; rep from *, end p3.
Rows 7 and 8—With A, repeat Rows 3 and 4.

Repeat Rows 1–8.

III. CAGE PATTERN

Multiple of 6 sts. Colors A and B.

Cast on with Color A and purl one row.

Row 1 (Right side)—With B, k5, * sl 2 wyib, k4; rep from *, end k1.
Row 2—With B, k5, * sl 2 wyif, k4; rep from *, end k1.
Row 3—With A, k1, * sl 1 wyib, k2; rep from *, end sl 1, k1.
Row 4—With A, p1, * sl 1 wyif, p2; rep from *, end sl 1, p1.
Row 5—With B, k2, * sl 2 wyib, k4; rep from *, end sl 2, k2.
Row 6—With B, k2, * sl 2 wyif, k4; rep from *, end sl 2, k2.
Rows 7 and 8—With A, repeat Rows 3 and 4.

Repeat Rows 1–8.

Vertical Chain

There are really two chains, interlocked with each other, in this pattern—a dark one on a light background, and a light one on a dark background. Thus the pattern is nothing but a simple variation on slipped vertical stripes.

Multiple of 8 sts plus 2. Colors A and B.

Cast on with Color A and purl one row.

NOTE: On all right-side (odd-numbered) rows, slip all sl-sts with yarn in *back*.

Row 1 (Right side)—With B, k3, * sl 1, k2, sl 1, k4; rep from *, end last repeat k3.
Row 2 and all other wrong-side rows—Purl (or knit) the same sts worked on previous row, with the same color; sl all the same sl-sts with yarn in *front*.
Row 3—With A, k1, sl 1, * k2, sl 2; rep from *, end k2, sl 1, k1.
Row 5—With B, repeat Row 1.
Row 7—With A, k2, * sl 1, k4, sl 1, k2; rep from *.
Row 9—With B, repeat Row 3.
Row 11—With A, repeat Row 7.
Row 12—See Row 2.

Repeat Rows 1–12.

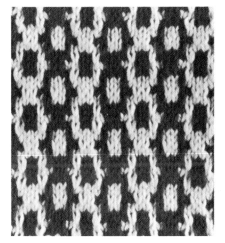

Vertical Chain

Fretted Mosaic

Fretted Mosaic

Multiple of 6 sts plus 2. Colors A and B.

NOTE: On all right-side rows, sl all sl-sts with yarn in *back*.

Rows 1 and 2—With A, knit.

Row 3 (Right side)—With B, k1, * sl 1 wyib, k5; rep from *, end k1.

Row 4 and all other wrong-side rows—Knit the same sts worked on previous row, with the same color; sl all the same sl-sts with yarn in *front*.

Row 5—With A, k2, * sl 1, k3, sl 1, k1; rep from *.

Row 7—With B, k1, * sl 1, k3, sl 1, k1; rep from *, end k1.

Row 9—With A, k6, * sl 1, k5; rep from *, end sl 1, k1.

Rows 11 and 12—With B, knit.

Row 13—With A, k4, * sl 1, k5; rep from *, end sl 1, k3.

Row 15—With B, * k3, sl 1, k1, sl 1; rep from *, end k2.

Row 17—With A, k2, * sl 1, k1, sl 1, k3; rep from *.

Row 19—With B, k3, * sl 1, k5; rep from *, end sl 1, k4.

Row 20—See Row 4.

Repeat Rows 1–20.

Fretted Band Pattern

Multiple of 6 sts plus 2. Colors A and B.

NOTE: On all right-side rows, sl all sl-sts with yarn in *back*.

VERSION I: BASIC FRETTED BAND

*Fretted Band Pattern, Version I
(Basic Fretted Band)*

Rows 1 and 2—With B, knit.

Row 3 (Right side)—With A, k6, * sl 1, k5; rep from *, end sl 1, k1.

Row 4 and all subsequent wrong-side rows—Knit the same sts worked on previous row, with the same color; sl all the same sl-sts with yarn in *front*.

Row 5—With B, k1, sl 1, * k3, sl 1, k1, sl 1; rep from *, end last repeat k2 instead of k1, sl 1.

Row 7—With A, k4, * sl 1, k1, sl 1, k3; rep from *, end last repeat k1.

Row 9—With B, k3, * sl 1, k1, sl 1, k3; rep from *, end last repeat k2.

Row 11—With A, k4, * sl 1, k5; rep from *, end sl 1, k3.

Row 12—See Row 4.

Repeat Rows 1–12.

VERSION II:
ALTERNATING FRETTED BAND

Rows 1 and 2—With A, knit.

Row 3 (Right side)—With B, k3, * sl 1, k5; rep from *, end sl 1, k4.

Row 4 and all subsequent wrong-side rows—See Row 4, above.

Rows 5 through 14—Repeat Rows 3 through 12 of Version I, above.

Row 15—With B, k1, * sl 1, k5; rep from *, end k1.

Rows 17 and 18—With A, knit.

Rows 19 through 36—Repeat Rows 1 through 18, reversing colors.

Repeat Rows 1–36.

Fretted Band Pattern, Version II
(Alternating Fretted Band)

Pin Box Pattern

To see how this clever pattern is constructed, plot it on graph paper. Put all the slip-stitches in their proper positions, and lo and behold, a diamond appears! Yet the motifs are quite evidently square—or nearly so.

Pin Box Pattern is actually made with pin stripes in a diamond formation. The diamond shapes *can* be seen on the wrong side. The pattern can be varied by knitting, instead of purling, the wrong-side rows; then the "boxes" will come out a little shorter and squarer, and the surface of the fabric will be rough and nubby.

Multiple of 12 sts plus 3. Colors A and B.

NOTE: On all odd-numbered (right-side) rows,
sl all sl-sts with yarn in *back*.

Pin Box Pattern

Row 1 (Right side)—With A, knit.

Row 2—With A, purl.

Row 3—With B, k1, * sl 1, k11; rep from *, end sl 1, k1.

Row 4 and all subsequent wrong-side rows—Purl all sts knitted on previous row, with same color; sl all the same sl-sts with yarn in *front*.

Row 5—With A, k2, * sl 1, k9, sl 1, k1; rep from *, end k1.

Row 7—With B, (k1, sl 1) twice, * k7, (sl 1, k1) twice, sl 1; rep from *, end k7, (sl 1, k1) twice.

Row 9—With A, k2, sl 1, k1, sl 1, * k5, (sl 1, k1) 3 times, sl 1; rep from *, end k5, sl 1, k1, sl 1, k2.

Row 11—With B, (k1, sl 1) 3 times, * k3, (sl 1, k1) 4 times, sl 1; rep from *, end k3, (sl 1, k1) 3 times.

Row 13—With A, k2, * sl 1, k1; rep from *, end k1.
Rows 15, 17, 19, 21, 23, and 25—Repeat Rows 11, 9, 7, 5, 3, and 1.
Row 27—With B, k7, * sl 1, k11; rep from *, end last repeat k7.
Row 29—With A, k6, * sl 1, k1, sl 1, k9; rep from *, end last repeat k6.
Row 31—With B, k5, * (sl 1, k1) twice, sl 1, k7; rep from *, end last repeat k5.
Row 33—With A, k4, * (sl 1, k1) 3 times, sl 1, k5; rep from *, end last repeat k4.
Row 35—With B, k3, * (sl 1, k1) 4 times, sl 1, k3; rep from *.
Row 37—With A, repeat Row 13.
Rows 39, 41, 43, 45, and 47—Repeat Rows 35, 33, 31, 29, and 27.
Row 48—See Row 4.

Repeat Rows 1–48.

Maze Pattern

Maze Pattern

Here is a fascinating arrangement of color stripes for a definitely unusual sweater or coat. It is surprisingly easy to knit.

Multiple of 14 sts plus 2. Colors A and B.

Cast on with Color A and purl one row.

NOTE: On all right-side (odd-numbered) rows, sl all sl-sts with yarn in *back*.

Row 1 (Right side)—With B, k1, * k7, (sl 1, k1) 3 times, sl 1; rep from *, end k1.
Row 2 and all other wrong-side rows—Purl all sts worked on previous row, with the same color; sl all the same sl-sts with yarn in *front*.
Row 3—With A, k1, * sl 1, k7, (sl 1, k1) 3 times; rep from *, end k1.
Row 5—With B, k2, * sl 1, k7, (sl 1, k1) 3 times; rep from *.
Row 7—With A, * (k1, sl 1) twice, k7, sl 1, k1, sl 1; rep from *, end k2.
Row 9—With B, k2, * sl 1, k1, sl 1, k7, (sl 1, k1) twice; rep from *.
Row 11—With A, * (k1, sl 1) 3 times, k7, sl 1; rep from *, end k2.
Row 13—With B, k1, * (k1, sl 1) 3 times, k7, sl 1; rep from *, end k1.
Row 15—With A, k1, * (sl 1, k1) 3 times, sl 1, k7; rep from *, end k1.
Row 17—With B, repeat Row 1.
Row 19—With A, * k7, (sl 1, k1) 3 times, sl 1; rep from *, end k2.
Row 21—With B, k6, * (sl 1, k1) 3 times, sl 1, k7; rep from *, end last repeat k3.
Row 23—With A, k5, * (sl 1, k1) 3 times, sl 1, k7; rep from *, end last repeat k4.
Row 25—With B, k4, * (sl 1, k1) 3 times, sl 1, k7; rep from *, end last repeat k5.
Row 27—With A, k3, * (sl 1, k1) 3 times, sl 1, k7; rep from *, end last repeat k6.
Row 29—With B, k2, * (sl 1, k1) 3 times, sl 1, k7; rep from *.
Row 31—With A, repeat Row 15.
Row 32—See Row 2.

Repeat Rows 1–32.

Assyrian Stripe Pattern

As Mosaics go, this one is simple to work because the directions are neither long nor complex—just repetitive. Yet it is a stunning pattern for any ski sweater, border, child's jacket, or hat.

Multiple of 16 sts plus 1. Colors A and B.

NOTE: On all right-side (odd-numbered) rows, sl all sl-sts with yarn in *back*.

Rows 1 and 2—With A, knit.
Row 3 (Right side)—With B, k1, * sl 1, k1; rep from *.
Row 4 and all other wrong-side rows—Knit (or purl) all the same sts worked on previous row, with the same color; sl all the same sl-sts with yarn in *front*.
Row 5—With A, k8, * sl 1, k15; rep from *, end sl 1, k8.
Row 7—With B, k2, * (sl 1, k1) twice, sl 1, k3; rep from *, end last repeat k2.
Row 9—With A, k7, * sl 3, k13; rep from *, end sl 3, k7.
Row 11—With B, k4, * sl 1, k7; rep from *, end sl 1, k4.
Row 13—With A, k5, * sl 1, k1, sl 3, k1, sl 1, k9; rep from *, end last repeat k5.
Rows 15, 17, 19, 21, 23 and 25—Repeat Rows 11, 9, 7, 5, 3, and 1.
Rows 27 through 51—Repeat Rows 1 through 25, reversing colors.
Row 52—With B, knit.

Repeat Rows 1–52.

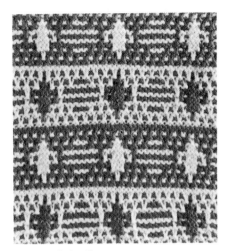

Assyrian Stripe Pattern

Stripes and Diamonds

Dotted diamonds appear to be embossed on a striped fabric in this pattern, which can be used to make a very handsome two-color garment. Various rearrangements of knits and purls can be applied to make different texture effects.

Multiple of 10 sts plus 1. Colors A and B.

Cast on with Color A and knit one row.

NOTE: On all right-side (odd-numbered) rows, sl all sl-sts wyib; on all wrong-side (even-numbered) rows, sl all sl-sts wyif.

Row 1 (Right side)—With B, k5, * sl 1, k9; rep from *, end sl 1, k5.
Row 2—With B, p5, * sl 1, p9; rep from *, end sl 1, p5.
Row 3—With A, knit.
Row 4—With A, k4, * p3, k7; rep from *, end p3, k4.
Row 5—With B, k4, * sl 1, k1, sl 1, k7; rep from *, end last repeat k4.
Row 6—With B, p4, * sl 1, k1, sl 1, p7; rep from *, end last repeat p4.

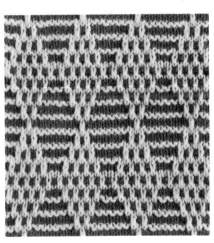

Stripes and Diamonds

Row 7—With A, knit.
Row 8—With A, k3, * p5, k5; rep from *, end p5, k3.
Row 9—With B, k3, * (sl 1, k1) twice, sl 1, k5; rep from *, end last repeat k3.
Row 10—With B, p3, * (sl 1, k1) twice, sl 1, p5; rep from *, end last repeat p3.
Row 11—With A, knit.
Row 12—With A, k2, * p7, k3; rep from *, end p7, k2.
Row 13—With B, k2, * (sl 1, k1) 3 times, sl 1, k3; rep from *, end last repeat k2.
Row 14—With B, p2, * (sl 1, k1) 3 times, sl 1, p3; rep from *, end last repeat p2.
Row 15—With A, knit.
Row 16—With A, purl.
Rows 17 and 18—With B, k1, * sl 1, k1; rep from *.
Rows 19 and 20—With A, repeat Rows 15 and 16.
Rows 21 and 22—With B, repeat Rows 13 and 14.
Rows 23 and 24—With A, repeat Rows 11 and 12.
Rows 25 and 26—With B, repeat Rows 9 and 10.
Rows 27 and 28—With A, repeat Rows 7 and 8.
Rows 29 and 30—With B, repeat Rows 5 and 6.
Rows 31 and 32—With A, repeat Rows 3 and 4.

Repeat Rows 1–32.

City Lights

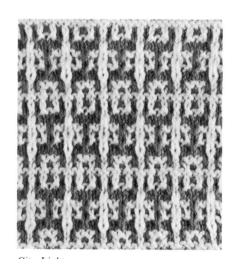

City Lights

Multiple of 6 sts plus 3. Colors A and B.

Cast on with Color A and purl one row.

NOTE: On all right-side (odd-numbered) rows, sl all sl-sts with yarn in *back*.

On all wrong-side (even-numbered) rows, sl all sl-sts with yarn in *front*.

Rows 1 and 2—With B, knit.
Row 3 (Right side)—With A, k2, * sl 1, k1; rep from *, end k1.
Row 4—With A, k2, * (sl 1, p1) twice, sl 1, k1; rep from *, end k1.
Row 5—With B, k3, * sl 1, k1, sl 1, k3; rep from *.
Row 6—With B, k3, * sl 1, p1, sl 1, k3; rep from *.
Row 7—With A, k4, * sl 1, k5; rep from *, end sl 1, k4.
Row 8—With A, p4, * sl 1, p5; rep from *, end sl 1, p4.
Row 9—With B, k1, * sl 1, k5; rep from *, end sl 1, k1.
Row 10—With B, k1, * sl 1, k2, p1, k2; rep from *, end sl 1, k1.
Row 11—With A, repeat Row 3.
Row 12—With A, p2, * (sl 1, k1) twice, sl 1, p1; rep from *, end p1.
Rows 13 and 14—With B, repeat Rows 9 and 10.
Rows 15 and 16—With A, repeat Rows 7 and 8.
Rows 17 and 18—With B, repeat Rows 5 and 6.
Rows 19 and 20—With A, repeat Rows 3 and 4.

Repeat Rows 1–20.

Four "Flying Cross" Mosaics:
Illusion Stripe, Dogtooth Cross,
Diagonal Chain, and Egyptian Cross

ABOVE, LEFT: *Illusion Stripe*
ABOVE, RIGHT: *Dogtooth Cross*
BELOW, LEFT: *Diagonal Chain*
BELOW, RIGHT: *Egyptian Cross*

The flying cross or four-armed cross (of which the swastika is one example) is an ancient and recurrent theme in geometric patterns the world over. Here it can be traced in four fascinating mosaic designs. In each, the basic motif is a small three-stitch square with a dot of contrasting color in the center and four "arms" proceeding from the corners. But this motif is very differently handled in each of the four.

The first two, Illusion Stripe and Dogtooth Cross, are similar but illustrate a small change that makes a big difference. Look at the light-colored shapes against the background of dark-colored ones, then at the dark-colored shapes against the background of the light-colored ones. In Illusion Stripe, both are alike—hence the "illusion". But in Dogtooth Cross the two colors form very different designs. The contrast between "dark" shapes and "light" shapes is even greater in the third and fourth patterns. Exchange the positions of dark and light rows, and these patterns will alter radically in their appearance. The last pattern, Egyptian Cross, begins and ends with plain knit rows and thus will make a very interesting border design as well as an allover pattern.

NOTES FOR ALL FOUR PATTERNS: On all right-side (odd-numbered) rows, slip all sl-sts with yarn in *back*. On all wrong-side (even-numbered) rows, knit (or purl) the same sts worked on previous row, with the same color; sl all the same sl-sts with yarn in *front*.

I. ILLUSION STRIPE

Multiple of 6 sts plus 2. Colors A and B.

Cast on with Color A and knit one row.

Row 1 (Right side)—With B, k1, * k5, sl 1; rep from *, end k1.
Row 3—With A, k1, * sl 1, k1, sl 1, k3; rep from *, end k1.
Row 5—With B, k4, * sl 1, k5; rep from *, end last repeat k3.
Row 7—With A, k3, * sl 1, k5; rep from *, end last repeat k4.
Row 9—With B, k4, * sl 1, k1, sl 1, k3; rep from *, end last repeat k1.
Row 11—With A, k1, * sl 1, k5; rep from *, end k1.
Row 12—See Notes.

Repeat Rows 1–12.

II. DOGTOOTH CROSS

Multiple of 6 sts plus 2. Colors A and B.

Cast on with Color A and knit one row.

Row 1 (Right side)—With B, * k5, sl 1; rep from *, end k2.
Row 3—With A, k2, * sl 1, k3, sl 1, k1; rep from *.
Row 5—With B, k3, * sl 1, k5; rep from *, end last repeat k4.
Row 7—With A, k2, * sl 1, k5; rep from *.
Row 9—With B, k1, * sl 1, k1; rep from *, end k1.
Row 11—With A, k1, * k5, sl 1; rep from *, end k1.
Row 12—See Notes.

Repeat Rows 1–12.

III. DIAGONAL CHAIN

Multiple of 8 sts plus 1. Colors A and B.

Cast on with Color A and knit one row.

Row 1 (Right side)—With B, * k7, sl 1; rep from *, end k1.
Row 3—With A, k2, * sl 1, k3; rep from *, end last repeat k2.
Row 5—With B, k1, * sl 1, k1, sl 1, k5; rep from *.
Row 7—With A, k4, * sl 1, k1, sl 1, k5; rep from *, end last repeat k2.
Row 9—With B, * k1, sl 1, k5, sl 1; rep from *, end k1.
Row 11—With A, k4, * sl 1, k3; rep from *, end k1.
Row 13—With B, k3, * sl 1, k7; rep from *, end last repeat k5.
Row 15—With A, k2, * sl 1, k5, sl 1, k1; rep from *, end sl 1, k6.
Row 16—See Notes.

Repeat Rows 1–16.

IV. EGYPTIAN CROSS

Multiple of 8 sts plus 3. Colors A and B.

Cast on with Color A and knit one row.

Row 1 (Right side)—With B, k1, * sl 1, k3, (sl 1, k1) twice; rep from *, end sl 1, k1.
Row 3—With A, k4, * sl 1, k3; rep from *, end last repeat k2.
Row 5—With B, k1, * sl 1, k1, sl 1, k5; rep from *, end sl 1, k1.
Row 7—With A, k4, * sl 1, k1, sl 1, k5; rep from *, end last repeat k4.
Row 9—With B, k1, * sl 1, k5, sl 1, k1; rep from *, end sl 1, k1.
Row 11—With A, k2, * sl 1, k3; rep from *, end k1.
Row 13—With B, k1, * (sl 1, k1) twice, sl 1, k3; rep from *, end sl 1, k1.
Rows 15 and 16—With A, knit.

Repeat Rows 1–16.

Miniature Mosaic

Multiple of 8 sts plus 3. Colors A and B.

Cast on with A and knit one row.

NOTE: On all right-side rows, sl all sl-sts with yarn in *back*.

Row 1 (Right side)—With B, k1, * sl 1, k7; rep from *, end sl 1, k1.

Row 2 and all other wrong-side rows—Knit (or purl) the same sts worked on previous row, with the same color; sl all the same sl-sts with yarn in *front*.

Row 3—With A, k4, * sl 1, k1, sl 1, k5; rep from *, end last repeat k4.

Row 5—With B, k3, * sl 1, k3; rep from *.

Row 7—With A, k2, * sl 1, k5, sl 1, k1; rep from *, end k1.

Row 9—With B, k5, * sl 1, k7; rep from *, end last repeat k5.

Rows 11 and 12—With A, repeat Rows 7 and 8.

Rows 13 and 14—With B, repeat Rows 5 and 6.

Rows 15 and 16—With A, repeat Rows 3 and 4.

Repeat Rows 1–16.

ABOVE: *Miniature Mosaic*
BELOW: *Pyramid*

Pyramid

Multiple of 14 sts plus 3. Colors A and B.

Cast on with A and knit one row.

NOTE: On all right-side rows, sl all sl-sts with yarn in *back*.

Row 1 (Right side)—With B, k8, * sl 1, k13; rep from *, end last repeat k8.

Row 2 and all other wrong-side rows—Knit (or purl) the same sts worked on previous row, with the same color; sl all the same sl-sts with yarn in *front*.

Row 3—With A, k2, * (sl 1, k1) twice, sl 1, k3, (sl 1, k1) 3 times; rep from *, end k1.

Row 5—With B, k7, * sl 1, k1, sl 1, k11; rep from *, end last repeat k7.

Row 7—With A, k2, * sl 1, k1, sl 1, k7, (sl 1, k1) twice; rep from *, end k1.

Row 9—With B, k5, * (sl 1, k1) 3 times, sl 1, k7; rep from *, end last repeat k5.

Row 11—With A, k2, * sl 1, k11, sl 1, k1; rep from *, end k1.

Row 13—With B, k3, * (sl 1, k1) 5 times, sl 1, k3; rep from *.

Row 15—With A, k1, * sl 1, k13; rep from *, end sl 1, k1.

Row 16—See Row 2.

Repeat Rows 1–16.

Lattice

Lattice

Multiple of 12 sts plus 3. Colors A and B.

Cast on with A and knit one row.

NOTE: On all right-side rows sl all sl-sts with yarn in *back*.

Row 1 (Right side)—With B, k1, * sl 1, k11; rep from *, end sl 1, k1.

Row 2 and all other wrong-side rows—Knit (or purl) the same sts worked on previous row, with the same color; sl all the same sl-sts with yarn in *front*.

Row 3—With A, k4, * (sl 1, k1) 3 times, sl 1, k5; rep from *, end last repeat k4.

Row 5—With B, k3, * sl 1, k7, sl 1, k3; rep from *.

Row 7—With A, k2, * sl 1, k3, sl 1, k1; rep from *, end k1.

Row 9—With B, k5, * sl 1, k3, sl 1, k7; rep from *, end last repeat k5.

Row 11—With A, k2, * sl 1, k1, sl 1, k5, (sl 1, k1) twice; rep from *, end k1.

Row 13—With B, k7, * sl 1, k11; rep from *, end last repeat k7.

Rows 15 and 16—With A, repeat Rows 11 and 12.

Rows 17 and 18—With B, repeat Rows 9 and 10.

Rows 19 and 20—With A, repeat Rows 7 and 8.

Rows 21 and 22—With B, repeat Rows 5 and 6.

Rows 23 and 24—With A, repeat Rows 3 and 4.

Repeat Rows 1–24.

Fancy Lattice

Fancy Lattice

Multiple of 14 sts plus 3. Colors A and B.

Cast on with A and knit one row.

NOTE: On all right-side rows sl all sl-sts with yarn in *back*.

Row 1 (Right side)—With B, k2, * (sl 1, k1) 3 times, k2, (sl 1, k1) 3 times; rep from *, end k1.

Row 2 and all other wrong-side rows—Knit (or purl) the same sts worked on previous row, with the same color; sl all the same sl-sts with yarn in *front*.

Row 3—With A, k7, * sl 1, k1, sl 1, k11; rep from *, end last repeat k7.

Row 5—With B, k1, sl 1, k1, * (sl 1, k4) twice, (sl 1, k1) twice; rep from *.

Row 7—With A, k4, * sl 1, k7, sl 1, k5; rep from *, end last repeat k4.

Row 9—With B, k5, * (sl 1, k1) 3 times, sl 1, k7; rep from *, end last repeat k5.

Row 11—With A, k1, * sl 1, k13; rep from *, end sl 1, k1.

Rows 13 and 14—With B, repeat Rows 9 and 10.

Rows 15 and 16—With A, repeat Rows 7 and 8.

Rows 17 and 18—With B, repeat Rows 5 and 6.

Rows 19 and 20—With A, repeat Rows 3 and 4.

Repeat Rows 1–20.

Greek Cross Medallion

Multiple of 14 sts plus 3. Colors A and B.

Cast on with A and knit one row.

NOTE: On all right-side rows, sl all sl-sts with yarn in *back*.

Row 1 (Right side)—With B, k2, * sl 1, k1, (sl 1, k3) twice, (sl 1, k1) twice; rep from *, end k1.

Row 2 and all other wrong-side rows—Knit (or purl) the same sts worked on previous row, with the same color; sl all the same sl-sts with yarn in *front*.

Row 3—With A, k5, * sl 1, k5, sl 1, k7; rep from *, end last repeat k5.

Row 5—With B, k2, * (sl 1, k3) 3 times, sl 1, k1; rep from *, end k1.

Row 7—With A, k3, * sl 1, k3, sl 1, k1, (sl 1, k3) twice; rep from *.

Row 9—With B, k4, * sl 1, k7, sl 1, k5; rep from *, end last repeat k4.

Row 11—With A, k1, * sl 1, k3, (sl 1, k1) 3 times, sl 1, k3; rep from *, end sl 1, k1.

Rows 13 and 14—With B, repeat Rows 9 and 10.

Rows 15 and 16—With A, repeat Rows 7 and 8.

Rows 17 and 18—With B, repeat Rows 5 and 6.

Rows 19 and 20—With A, repeat Rows 3 and 4.

Repeat Rows 1–20.

Greek Cross Medallion

Key and Basket Pattern

Multiple of 16 sts plus 3. Colors A and B.

Cast on with A and knit one row.

NOTE: On all right-side rows, sl all sl-sts with yarn in *back*.

Row 1 (Right side)—With B, k1, * (k1, sl 1, k3, sl 1) twice, k3, sl 1; rep from *, end k2.

Row 2 and all other wrong-side rows—Knit (or purl) the same sts worked on previous row, with the same color; sl all the same sl-sts with yarn in *front*.

Row 3—With A, k1, * sl 1, k3; rep from *, end sl 1, k1.

Row 5—With B, k4, * sl 1, k1, (sl 1, k3) twice, sl 1, k5; rep from *, end last repeat k4.

Row 7—With A, k2, * sl 2, k3, (sl 1, k3) twice, sl 2, k1; rep from *, end k1.

Row 9—With B, k4, * (sl 1, k3) twice, sl 1, k1, sl 1, k5; rep from *, end last repeat k4.

Row 11—With A, repeat Row 3.

Key and Basket Pattern

Row 13—With B, k2, * (sl 1, k3) twice, sl 1, k1, sl 1, k3, sl 1, k1; rep from *, end k1.

Row 15—With A, k3, * sl 1, k3; rep from *.

Row 17—With B, k2, * (sl 1, k1, sl 1, k3) twice, sl 1, k3; rep from *, end k1.

Row 19—With A, repeat Row 3.

Row 21—With B, k4, * sl 1, k1, sl 1, k5, (sl 1, k3) twice; rep from *, end last repeat k2.

Row 23—With A, k3, * sl 1, k3, sl 2, k1, sl 2, k3, sl 1, k3; rep from *.

Row 25—With B, k2, * sl 1, k3, sl 1, k5, sl 1, k1, sl 1, k3; rep from *, end k1.

Row 27—With A, repeat Row 3.

Row 29—With B, k4, * (sl 1, k3, sl 1, k1) twice, sl 1, k3; rep from *, end last repeat k2.

Row 31—With A, repeat Row 15.

Row 32—See Row 2.

Repeat Rows 1–32.

Oblong Medallion

Oblong Medallion

Multiple of 24 sts plus 3. Colors A and B.

Cast on with A and knit one row.

NOTE: On all right-side rows, sl all sl-sts with yarn in *back*.

Row 1 (Right side)—With B, k5, * sl 1, k4, sl 1, k5, sl 1, k4, sl 1, k7; rep from *, end last repeat k5.

Row 2 and all other wrong-side rows—Knit (or purl) the same sts worked on previous row, with the same color; sl all the same sl-sts with yarn in *front*.

Row 3—With A, k6, * sl 1, k4, sl 1, k3, sl 1, k4, sl 1, k9; rep from *, end last repeat k6.

Row 5—With B, k2, * (sl 1, k4) twice, sl 1, k1, sl 1, (k4, sl 1) twice, k1; rep from *, end k1.

Row 7—With A, k3, * sl 1, k4, sl 1, k9, sl 1, k4, sl 1, k3; rep from *.

Row 9—With B, k4, * sl 1, k4, sl 1, k7, sl 1, k4, sl 1, k5; rep from *, end last repeat k4.

Row 11—With A, k1, * sl 1, k3, sl 1, k4, (sl 1, k1) 3 times, sl 1, k4, sl 1, k3; rep from *, end sl 1, k1.

Rows 13 and 14—With B, repeat Rows 9 and 10.

Rows 15 and 16—With A, repeat Rows 7 and 8.

Rows 17 and 18—With B, repeat Rows 5 and 6.

Rows 19 and 20—With A, repeat Rows 3 and 4.

Rows 21 and 22—With B, repeat Rows 1 and 2.

Row 23—With A, k2, sl 1, k1, * sl 1, k4, (sl 1, k3) twice, sl 1, k4, (sl 1, k1) 3 times; rep from *, end sl 1, k4, (sl 1, k3) twice, sl 1, k4, sl 1, k1, sl 1, k2.

Row 24—See Row 2.

Repeat Rows 1–24.

Double Medallion

Multiple of 22 sts plus 3. Colors A and B.

Cast on with A and knit one row.

NOTE: On all right-side rows, sl all sl-sts with yarn in *back*.

Row 1 (Right side)—With B, k3, * (sl 1, k8) twice, sl 1, k3; rep from*.

Row 2 and all other wrong-side rows—Knit (or purl) the same sts worked on previous row, with the same color; sl all the same sl-sts with yarn in *front*.

Row 3—With A, k4, * (sl 1, k1) 3 times, k6, (sl 1, k1) 3 times, k4; rep from *, end last repeat k3.

Row 5—With B, k9, * sl 1, k5, sl 1, k15; rep from *, end last repeat k9.

Row 7—With A, (k1, sl 1) 3 times, * k4, sl 1, k3, sl 1, k4, (sl 1, k1) 4 times, sl 1; rep from *, end k4, sl 1, k3, sl 1, k4, (sl 1, k1) 3 times.

Row 9—With B, k6, * sl 1, k4, sl 1, k1, sl 1, k4, sl 1, k9; rep from *, end last repeat k6.

Row 11—With A, k2, * sl 1, k4, sl 1, k9, sl 1, k4, sl 1, k1; rep from *, end k1.

Row 13—With B, k3, * sl 1, k4, (sl 1, k1) 4 times, sl 1, k4, sl 1, k3; rep from*.

Row 15—With A, k4, * sl 1, k15, sl 1, k5; rep from *, end last repeat k4.

Rows 17 and 18—With B, repeat Rows 13 and 14.
Rows 19 and 20—With A, repeat Rows 11 and 12.
Rows 21 and 22—With B, repeat Rows 9 and 10.
Rows 23 and 24—With A, repeat Rows 7 and 8.
Rows 25 and 26—With B, repeat Rows 5 and 6.
Rows 27 and 28—With A, repeat Rows 3 and 4.

Repeat Rows 1–28.

Double Medallion

Fancy Parallelogram

Multiple of 16 sts plus 2. Colors A and B.

Cast on with A and knit one row.

NOTE: On all right-side rows, sl all sl-sts with yarn in *back*.

Row 1 (Right side)—With B, k1, * k4, sl 1, k11; rep from *, end k1.

Row 2 and all other wrong-side rows—Knit (or purl) the same sts worked on previous row, with the same color; sl all the same sl-sts with yarn in *front*.

Fancy Parallelogram

Row 3—With A, k1, * (k3, sl 1) twice, (k1, sl 1) 3 times, k2; rep from *, end k1.

Row 5—With B, k1, * k2, sl 1, k3, sl 1, k7, sl 1, k1; rep from *, end k1.

Row 7—With A, k1, * k1, (sl 1, k3) twice, sl 1, k1, sl 1, k3, sl 1; rep from *, end k1.

Row 9—With B, k1, * k4, (sl 1, k3) 3 times; rep from *, end k1.

Row 11—With A, k1, * (k3, sl 1) 3 times, k4; rep from *, end k1.

Row 13—With B, k1, * sl 1, k3, sl 1, k1, (sl 1, k3) twice, sl 1, k1; rep from *, end k1.

Row 15—With A, k1, * k1, sl 1, k7, sl 1, k3, sl 1, k2; rep from *, end k1.

Row 17—With B, k1, * k2, (sl 1, k1) 3 times, (sl 1, k3) twice; rep from *, end k1.

Row 19—With A, k1, * k11, sl 1, k4; rep from *, end k1.

Row 20—See Row 2.

Repeat Rows 1–20.

Crown Chevron

Crown Chevron

Multiple of 18 sts plus 3. Colors A and B.

Cast on with Color A and purl one row.

NOTE: On all right-side (odd-numbered) rows, sl all sl-sts with yarn in *back*.

Row 1 (Right side)—With B, k2, * sl 1, k2, (sl 1, k4) twice, sl 1, k2, sl 1, k1; rep from *, end k1.

Row 2 and all other wrong-side rows—Purl (or knit) the same sts worked on previous row, with the same color; sl all the same sl-sts with yarn in *front*.

Row 3—With A, k1, * sl 1, k4, sl 1, k1, sl 1, k3, sl 1, k1, sl 1, k4; rep from *, end sl 1, k1.

Row 5—With B, k3, * sl 1, k5, sl 1, k1, sl 1, k5, sl 1, k3; rep from *.

Row 7—With A, k2, * (sl 1, k1) twice, sl 1, k7, (sl 1, k1) 3 times; rep from *, end k1.

Row 9—With B, k7, * (sl 1, k1) 3 times, sl 1, k11; rep from *, end last repeat k7.

Row 11—With A, k2, * sl 1, k1, (sl 1, k5) twice, (sl 1, k1) twice; rep from *, end k1.

Row 13—With B, k5, * sl 2, k7; rep from *, end last repeat k5.

Row 15—With A, k1, * sl 1, k5, (sl 1, k1) 3 times, sl 1, k5; rep from *, end sl 1, k1.

Row 17—With B, k2, * sl 1, k1, sl 1, k11, (sl 1, k1) twice; rep from *, end k1.

Row 19—With A, k5, * (sl 1, k1) 5 times, sl 1, k7; rep from *, end last repeat k5.

Row 21—With B, k2, * sl 1, k5, sl 1, k3, sl 1, k5, sl 1, k1; rep from *, end k1.

Row 23—With A, k3, * sl 1, k1, (sl 1, k4) twice, sl 1, k1, sl 1, k3; rep from *.

Row 25—With B, k1, * sl 1, k4, sl 1, k2, sl 1, k1, sl 1, k2, sl 1, k4; rep from *, end sl 1, k1.

Row 27—With A, knit.

Row 28—With A, purl (or knit).

Repeat Rows 1–28.

Yang and Yin, or Endless Branch

Multiple of 20 sts plus 2. Colors A and B.

Cast on with A and purl one row.

NOTE: On all right-side rows, sl all sl-sts with yarn in *back*.

Row 1 (Right side)—With B, k1, * k2, sl 2, k6, sl 2, k8; rep from *, end k1.

Row 2 and all other wrong-side rows—Purl the same sts worked on previous row, with the same color; sl all the same sl-sts with yarn in *front*.

Row 3—With A, k1, * k4, (sl 2, k6) twice; rep from *, end k1.

Row 5—With B, k1, * sl 2, k4, sl 2, k2; rep from *, end k1.

Row 7—With A, k1, * k2, (sl 2, k4) 3 times; rep from *, end k1.

Row 9—With B, k1, * k4, sl 2, k6, sl 2, k4, sl 2; rep from *, end k1.

Row 11—With A, k1, * sl 2, k4, sl 2, k2; rep from *, end k1.

Row 13—With B, k1, * k2, sl 2, k10, sl 2, k4; rep from *, end k1.

Row 15—With A, k1, * sl 2, k10, sl 2, k6; rep from *, end k1.

Row 17—With B, k1, * k4, sl 2, k2, sl 2; rep from *, end k1.

Row 19—With A, k1, * k2, sl 2, k6, sl 2, k4, sl 2, k2; rep from *, end k1.

Row 21—With B, k1, * (sl 2, k4) twice, sl 2, k6; rep from *, end k1.

Row 23—With A, k1, * k4, sl 2, k2, sl 2; rep from *, end k1.

Row 24—See Row 2.

Repeat Rows 1–24.

Yang and Yin, or Endless Branch

Fancy Chevron

Multiple of 26 sts plus 3. Colors Á and B.

Cast on with A and purl one row.

NOTE: On all right-side rows, sl all sl-sts with yarn in *back*. On all wrong-side rows, sl all sl-sts with yarn in *front*.

Row 1 (Right side)—With B, k9, * sl 2, k7, sl 2, k15; rep from *, end last repeat k9.

Row 2—With B, k9, * sl 2, p7, sl 2, k15; rep from *, end last repeat k9.

Row 3—With A, k2, * (sl 1, k1) twice, sl 1, k4, sl 2, k3, sl 2, k4, (sl 1, k1) 3 times; rep from *, end k1.

Row 4—With A, k2, * (sl 1, k1) twice, sl 1, p4, sl 2, k3, sl 2, p4, (sl 1, k1) 3 times; rep from *, end k1.

Row 5—With B, k7, * sl 2, k4, sl 1, k1, sl 1, k4, sl 2, k11; rep from *, end last repeat k7.

Fancy Chevron

Row 6—With B, k7, * sl 2, p4, sl 1, k1, sl 1, p4, sl 2, k11; rep from *, end last repeat k7.

Row 7—With A, k2, * sl 1, k1, sl 1, k4, sl 2, k7, sl 2, k4, (sl 1, k1) twice; rep from *, end k1.

Row 8—With A, k2, * sl 1, k1, sl 1, p4, sl 2, k7, sl 2, p4, (sl 1, k1) twice; rep from *, end k1.

Row 9—With B, k5, * sl 2, k4, (sl 1, k1) 3 times, sl 1, k4, sl 2, k7; rep from *, end last repeat k5.

Row 10—With B, k5, * sl 2, p4, (sl 1, k1) 3 times, sl 1, p4, sl 2, k7; rep from *, end last repeat k5.

Row 11—With A, k2, * sl 1, k4, sl 2, k11, sl 2, k4, sl 1, k1; rep from *, end k1.

Row 12—With A, k2, * sl 1, p4, sl 2, k11, sl 2, p4, sl 1, k1; rep from *, end k1.

Row 13—With B, k3, * sl 2, k4, (sl 1, k1) 5 times, sl 1, k4, sl 2, k3; rep from *.

Row 14—With B, k3, * sl 2, p4, (sl 1, k1) 5 times, sl 1, p4, sl 2, k3; rep from *.

Row 15—With A, k5, * sl 2, k15, sl 2, k7; rep from *, end last repeat k5.

Row 16—With A, p5, * sl 2, k15, sl 2, p7; rep from *, end last repeat p5.

Row 17—With B, k2, * sl 1, k8, sl 2, k3, sl 2, k8, sl 1, k1; rep from *, end k1.

Row 18—With B, k2, * sl 1, p8, sl 2, p3, sl 2, p8, sl 1, k1; rep from *, end k1.

Row 19—With A, k3, * sl 2, k8, sl 1, k1, sl 1, k8, sl 2, k3; rep from *.

Row 20—With A, p3, * sl 2, p8, sl 1, k1, sl 1, p8, sl 2, p3; rep from *.

Repeat Rows 1–20.

Divided Diamond

Divided Diamond

Multiple of 22 sts plus 2. Colors A and B.

Cast on with A and knit one row.

NOTE: On all right-side rows, sl all sl-sts with yarn in *back*.

Row 1 (Right side)—With B, k1, * k10, sl 1, k3, sl 1, k7; rep from *, end k1.

Row 2 and all other wrong-side rows—Knit (or purl) the same sts worked on previous row, with the same color; sl all the same sl-sts with yarn in *front*.

Row 3—With A, k1, * (k1, sl 1) 4 times, k3, sl 1, k1, sl 1, k3, (sl 1, k1) twice, sl 1; rep from *, end k1.

Row 5—With B, k1, * k8, (sl 1, k3) twice, sl 1, k5; rep from *, end k1.

Row 7—With A, k1, * (k1, sl 1) 3 times, k3, sl 1, k5, sl 1, k3, sl 1, k1, sl 1; rep from *, end k1.

Row 9—With B, k1, * k6, sl 1, k3, (sl 1, k1) twice, (sl 1, k3) twice; rep from *, end k1.

Row 11—With A, k1, * (k1, sl 1) twice, k3, sl 1, k9, sl 1, k3, sl 1; rep from *, end k1.

Row 13—With B, k1, * k4, sl 1, k3, (sl 1, k1) 4 times, sl 1, k3, sl 1, k1; rep from *, end k1.

Row 15—With A, k1, * k1, sl 1, k3, sl 1, k13, sl 1, k2; rep from *, end k1.

Row 17—With B, k1, * sl 1, k1, sl 1, k3, (sl 1, k1) 6 times, sl 1, k3; rep from *, end k1.

Row 19—With A, k1, * k3, sl 1, k17, sl 1; rep from *, end k1.

Row 21—With B, k1, * k2, sl 1, k17, sl 1, k1; rep from *, end k1.

Row 23—With A, k1, * k1, sl 1, k3, (sl 1, k1) 6 times, sl 1, k3, sl 1; rep from *, end k1.

Row 25—With B, k1, * sl 1, k3, sl 1, k13, sl 1, k3; rep from *, end k1.

Row 27—With A, k1, * (k3, sl 1) twice, (k1, sl 1) 4 times, k3, sl 1, k2; rep from *, end k1.

Row 29—With B, k1, * sl 1, k1, sl 1, k3, sl 1, k9, sl 1, k3, sl 1, k1; rep from *, end k1.

Row 31—With A, k1, * k5, sl 1, k3, (sl 1, k1) twice, sl 1, k3, sl 1, k4; rep from *, end k1.

Row 33—With B, k1, * (sl 1, k1) twice, sl 1, k3, sl 1, k5, sl 1, k3, (sl 1, k1) twice; rep from *, end k1.

Row 35—With A, k1, * k7, (sl 1, k3) twice, sl 1, k6; rep from *, end k1.

Row 37—With B, k1, * (sl 1, k1) 3 times, sl 1, k3, sl 1, k1, sl 1, k3, (sl 1, k1) 3 times; rep from *, end k1.

Row 39—With A, k1, * k9, sl 1, k3, sl 1, k8; rep from *, end k1.

Row 40—See Row 2.

Repeat Rows 1–40.

Trellis Diamond

Multiple of 30 sts plus 3. Colors A and B.

Cast on with A and knit one row.

NOTE: On all right-side rows, sl all sl-sts with yarn in *back*.

Row 1 (Right side)—With B, k8, * (sl 1, k3) 4 times, sl 1, k13; rep from *, end last repeat k8.

Row 2 and all other wrong-side rows—Knit (or purl) the same sts worked on previous row, with the same color; sl all the same sl-sts with yarn in *front*.

Row 3—With A, k1, * (sl 1, k3) 3 times, sl 1, k1, (sl 1, k3) 4 times; rep from *, end sl 1, k1.

Row 5—With B, k6, * (sl 1, k3) 5 times, sl 1, k9; rep from *, end last repeat k6.

Row 7—With A, k1, sl 1, k1, * (sl 1, k3) 3 times, sl 1, k1, (sl 1, k3) 3 times, (sl 1, k1) twice; rep from *.

Row 9—With B, k4, * (sl 1, k3) 6 times, sl 1, k5; rep from *, end last repeat k4.

Trellis Diamond

MOSAIC PATTERNS   121

Row 11—With A, k1, * (sl 1, k3) 3 times, sl 1, k5, (sl 1, k3) 3 times; rep from *, end sl 1, k1.

Row 13—With B, k2, * (sl 1, k3) 3 times, (sl 1, k1) twice, (sl 1, k3) 3 times, sl 1, k1; rep from *, end k1.

Row 15—With A, k3, * (sl 1, k3) twice, sl 1, k9, (sl 1, k3) 3 times; rep from *.

Row 17—With B, k2, * sl 1, k1, (sl 1, k3) 7 times; rep from *, end k1.

Row 19—With A, k1, * (sl 1, k3) twice, sl 1, k13, (sl 1, k3) twice; rep from *, end sl 1, k1.

Row 21—With B, k4, * (sl 1, k3) 6 times, sl 1, k1, sl 1, k3; rep from *, end last repeat k2.

Rows 23 and 24—With A, repeat Rows 15 and 16.

Rows 25 and 26—With B, repeat Rows 13 and 14.

Rows 27 and 28—With A, repeat Rows 11 and 12.

Rows 29 and 30—With B, repeat Rows 9 and 10.

Rows 31 and 32—With A, repeat Rows 7 and 8.

Rows 33 and 34—With B, repeat Rows 5 and 6.

Row 35—With A, k1, * (sl 1, k3) 4 times, sl 1, k1, (sl 1, k3) 3 times; rep from *, end sl 1, k1.

Row 36—See Row 2.

Repeat Rows 1–36.

Arabic Block

Arabic Block

This is a slip-stitch adaptation of an ancient Arabic design. The method here has a touch of novelty; in order that the same strand of yarn can be used all the way across each row, the left-hand half of the pattern is always two rows behind the right-hand half. Thus a positive-and-negative checkered effect is achieved, and the blocks of color can be alternated without picking up new strands of yarn in mid-row.

Multiple of 54 sts plus 2. Colors A and B.

Cast on with A and knit one row.

NOTE: On all right-side rows, sl all sl-sts with yarn in *back*.

Row 1 (Right side)—With B, k1, * [(sl 1, k1) 10 times, sl 1, k3, sl 1, k1, sl 1], k23, (sl 1, k1) twice; rep from *, end k1.

Row 2 and all other wrong-side rows—Knit (or purl) the same sts worked on previous row, with the same color; sl all the same sl-sts with yarn in *front*.

Row 3—With A, k1, * [k7, sl 1, k13, sl 1, k3, sl 1, k1], rep [to] of Row 1; rep from *, end k1.

Row 5—With B, k1, * [(sl 1, k1) twice, sl 1, k5, (sl 1, k1) 4 times, (sl 1, k3) twice, sl 1], rep [to] of Row 3; rep from *, end k1.

Row 7—With A, k1, * [k5, sl 1, k3, sl 1, k9, (sl 1, k3) twice], rep [to] of Row 5; rep from *, end k1.

Row 9—With B, k1, * [(sl 1, k1, sl 1, k3) twice, (sl 1, k1) twice, (sl 1, k3) twice, sl 1, k1, sl 1], rep [to] of Row 7; rep from *, end k1.

Row 11—With A, k1, * [k3, sl 1, k7, sl 1, k5, sl 1, k3, sl 1, k5], rep [to] of Row 9; rep from *, end k1.

Row 13—With B, k1, * [sl 1, k3, (sl 1, k1) 3 times, (sl 1, k3) 3 times, (sl 1, k1) twice, sl 1], rep [to] of Row 11; rep from *, end k1.

Row 15—With A, k1, * [k3, sl 1, k7, (sl 1, k3) twice, sl 1, k7], rep [to] of Row 13; rep from *, end k1.

Row 17—With B, k1, * [(sl 1, k1, sl 1, k3) twice, (sl 1, k3) twice, (sl 1, k1) 3 times, sl 1], rep [to] of Row 15; rep from *, end k1.

Row 19—With A, k1, * [k5, (sl 1, k3) 3 times, sl 1, k9], rep [to] of Row 17; rep from *, end k1.

Row 21—With B, k1, * [(sl 1, k1) twice, sl 1, k5, (sl 1, k3) twice, (sl 1, k1) 4 times, sl 1], rep [to] of Row 19; rep from *, end k1.

Row 23—With A, k1, * [k7, (sl 1, k3) 3 times, sl 1, k7], rep [to] of Row 21; rep from *, end k1.

Row 25—With B, k1, * [(sl 1, k1) 4 times, (sl 1, k3) twice, sl 1, k5, (sl 1, k1) twice, sl 1], rep [to] of Row 23; rep from *, end k1.

Row 27—With A, k1, * [k9, (sl 1, k3) 3 times, sl 1, k5], rep [to] of Row 25; rep from *, end k1.

Row 29—With B, k1, * [(sl 1, k1) 3 times, (sl 1, k3) 3 times, sl 1, k1, sl 1, k3, sl 1, k1, sl 1], rep [to] of Row 27; rep from *, end k1.

Row 31—With A, k1, * [k7, (sl 1, k3) twice, sl 1, k7, sl 1, k3], rep [to] of Row 29; rep from *, end k1.

Row 33—With B, k1, * [(sl 1, k1) twice, (sl 1, k3) 3 times, (sl 1, k1) 3 times, sl 1, k3, sl 1], rep [to] of Row 31; rep from *, end k1.

Row 35—With A, k1, * [k5, sl 1, k3, sl 1, k5, sl 1, k7, sl 1, k3], rep [to] of Row 33; rep from *, end k1.

Row 37—With B, k1, * [sl 1, k1, (sl 1, k3) twice, (sl 1, k1) twice, sl 1, (k3, sl 1, k1, sl 1) twice], rep [to] of Row 35; rep from *, end k1.

Row 39—With A, k1, * [(k3, sl 1) twice, k9, sl 1, k3, sl 1, k5], rep [to] of Row 37; rep from *, end k1.

Row 41—With B, k1, * [(sl 1, k3) twice, (sl 1, k1) 4 times, sl 1, k5, (sl 1, k1) twice, sl 1], rep [to] of Row 39; rep from *, end k1.

Row 43—With A, k1, * [k1, sl 1, k3, sl 1, k13, sl 1, k7], rep [to] of Row 41; rep from *, end k1.

Row 45—With B, k1, * [sl 1, k1, sl 1, k3, (sl 1, k1) 10 times, sl 1], rep [to] of Row 43; rep from *, end k1.

Row 47—With A, k1, * [(k1, sl 1) twice, k23], rep [to] of Row 45; rep from *, end k1.

Row 49—With B, k1, * k23, (sl 1, k1) twice, rep [to] of Row 47; rep from *, end k1.

Row 50—See Row 2.

Rows 51 through 100—Repeat Rows 1 through 50, reversing colors; Color A for 51 and 52, Color B for 53 and 54, etc.

Repeat Rows 1–100.

Flare

Flare

Multiple of 55 sts plus 2. Colors A and B.

NOTE: On all right-side rows, sl all sl-sts with yarn in *back*.

Row 1 (Right side)—With A, knit.

Row 2—With A, knit.

Row 3—With B, k1, * k18, sl 1, k3, sl 1, k2, (sl 1, k1) twice, sl 1, k2, sl 1, k3, sl 1, k18; rep from *, end k1.

Row 4 and all other wrong-side rows—Knit (or purl) the same sts worked on previous row, with the same color; sl all the same sl-sts with yarn in *front*.

Row 5—With A, k1, * (sl 1, k1) 7 times, sl 1, k4, sl 1, k3, sl 1, k2, sl 1, k1, sl 1, k2, sl 1, k3, sl 1, k4, (sl 1, k1) 7 times, sl 1; rep from *, end k1.

Row 7—With B, k1, * k15, sl 1, k4, sl 1, k3, (sl 1, k2) twice, sl 1, k3, sl 1, k4, sl 1, k15; rep from *, end k1.

Row 9—With A, k1, * (k1, sl 1) 6 times, k4, sl 2, k3, sl 2, k2, sl 2, k1, sl 2, k2, sl 2, k3, sl 2, k4, (sl 1, k1) 6 times; rep from *, end k1.

Row 11—With B, k1, * k12, sl 1, k5, sl 1, k4, sl 1, (k3, sl 1) twice, k4, sl 1, k5, sl 1, k12; rep from *, end k1.

Row 13—With A, k1, * (sl 1, k1) 4 times, sl 1, k4, sl 1, k1, sl 1, k3, sl 1, k1, sl 1, k2, (sl 1, k1) 3 times, sl 1, k2, sl 1, k1, sl 1, k3, sl 1, k1, sl 1, k4, (sl 1, k1) 4 times, sl 1; rep from *, end k1.

Row 15—With B, k1, * k9, sl 1, k6, sl 1, k5, sl 1, (k4, sl 1) twice, k5, sl 1, k6, sl 1, k9; rep from *, end k1.

Row 17—With A, k1, * (k1, sl 1) 3 times, k4, sl 1, k1, sl 2, k3, sl 1, k1, sl 2, k2, sl 1, (k1, sl 2) twice, k1, sl 1, k2, sl 2, k1, sl 1, k3, sl 2, k1, sl 1, k4, (sl 1, k1) 3 times; rep from *, end k1.

Row 19—With B, k1, * k6, sl 1, k7, sl 1, k6, sl 1, (k5, sl 1) twice, k6, sl 1, k7, sl 1, k6; rep from *, end k1.

Row 21—With A, k1, * sl 1, k1, sl 1, k4, (sl 1, k1) twice, sl 1, k3, (sl 1, k1) twice, sl 1, k2, (sl 1, k1) 5 times, sl 1, k2, (sl 1, k1) twice, sl 1, k3, (sl 1, k1) twice, sl 1, k4, sl 1, k1, sl 1; rep from *, end k1.

Row 23—With B, k1, * k3, sl 1, k8, sl 1, k7, sl 1, (k6, sl 1) twice, k7, sl 1, k8, sl 1, k3; rep from *, end k1.

Row 25—With A, k1, * k4, (sl 1, k1) twice, sl 2, k3, (sl 1, k1) twice, sl 2, k2, (sl 1, k1) twice, sl 2, k1, sl 2, (k1, sl 1) twice, k2, sl 2, (k1, sl 1) twice, k3, sl 2, (k1, sl 1) twice, k4; rep from *, end k1.

Row 27—With B, k1, * sl 1, k9, sl 1, k8, (sl 1, k7) twice, sl 1, k8, sl 1, k9, sl 1; rep from *, end k1.

Rows 29 and 30—With A, knit.

Rows 31 and 32—With B, knit.

Rows 33–58—Repeat Rows 3–28, reversing colors.

Rows 59 and 60—With B, knit.

Repeat Rows 1–60.

Odin's Eagles

As its name implies, this pattern is derived from traditional Scandinavian designs. A kinship can be seen between the "eagle" motifs and those of the Crown Chevron. Odin's Eagles make a splendid border design when the pattern rows 1 through 42 are worked once, with Rows 43 and 44 knit plain with Color A. This pattern also makes beautiful cushions and handbags; articles like these can be worked with the required large multiple of stitches without any adjustment of the pattern to a given size. However, the knitter should remember that a mosaic pattern *can* be worked on any number of stitches, even if the final repeats end somewhere in the middle of the directions—so large multiples present no problem in patterns of this type.

Odin's Eagles

Multiple of 32 sts plus 3. Colors A and B.

Cast on with Color A and knit one row.

NOTE: On all right-side (odd-numbered) rows, slip all sl-sts with yarn in *back*.

Row 1 (Right side)—With B, k2, * (sl 1, k1, sl 1, k3) twice, (sl 1, k1) 3 times, (sl 1, k3, sl 1, k1) twice, sl 1, k1; rep from *, end k1.

Row 2 and all other wrong-side rows—Knit (or purl) the same sts worked on previous row, with the same color; sl all the same sl-sts with yarn in *front*.

Row 3—With A, k7, * sl 1, k3, sl 1, k11; rep from *, end last repeat k7.

Row 5—With B, k5, * sl 2, k5, sl 2, k6, sl 1, k1, sl 1, k5, sl 1, k1, sl 1, k6; rep from *, end last repeat k4.

Row 7—With A, k2, * sl 1, k1, (sl 1, k4) twice, (sl 1, k1) twice, (sl 1, k6) twice, sl 1, k1; rep from *, end k1.

Row 9—With B, * k7, sl 1, k3, sl 1, k7, (sl 1, k1) twice, sl 1, k3, (sl 1, k1) twice, sl 1; rep from *, end k3.

Row 11—With A, k2, * (sl 1, k1) 7 times, sl 1, k7, sl 1, k1, sl 1, k7; rep from *, end k1.

Row 13—With B, k1, * sl 1, k15, (sl 1, k1) twice, sl 1, k7, (sl 1, k1) twice; rep from *, end sl 1, k1.

Row 15—With A, k4, * (sl 1, k1) 5 times, sl 1, k7, sl 1, k5, sl 1, k7; rep from *, end last repeat k6.

Row 17—With B, k1, * sl 1, k1, sl 1, k11, sl 2, k1, sl 2, k11, sl 1, k1; rep from *, end sl 1, k1.

Row 19—With A, k8, * sl 1, k1, sl 1, k6, sl 1, k2, (sl 1, k4) twice, sl 1, k9; rep from *, end last repeat k4.

Row 21—With B, k7, * sl 1, k3, (sl 1, k1) twice, sl 1, k3, sl 1, k19; rep from *, end last repeat k15.

Row 23—With A, k1, * sl 1, k4, sl 1, k2, sl 1, k6, sl 1, k1, sl 1, k9, sl 1, k4; rep from *, end sl 1, k1.

Row 25—With B, k7, * sl 2, k1, sl 2, k11, (sl 1, k1) twice, sl 1, k11; rep from *, end last repeat k7.

Row 27—With A, k4, * sl 1, k7, (sl 1, k1) 5 times, sl 1, k7, sl 1, k5; rep from *, end last repeat k4.

Row 29—With B, k5, * (sl 1, k1) twice, sl 1, k15, (sl 1, k1) twice, sl 1, k7; rep from *, end last repeat k5.

Row 31—With A, k2, * sl 1, k7, (sl 1, k1) 7 times, sl 1, k7, sl 1, k1; rep from *, end k1.

Row 33—With B, k3, * (sl 1, k1) twice, sl 1, k7, sl 1, k3, sl 1, k7, (sl 1, k1) twice, sl 1, k3; rep from *.

Row 35—With A, k1, * sl 1, k6, (sl 1, k1) twice, (sl 1, k4) twice, (sl 1, k1) twice, sl 1, k6; rep from *, end sl 1, k1.

Row 37—With B, k4, * sl 1, k1, sl 1, k6, sl 2, k5, sl 2, k6, sl 1, k1, sl 1, k5; rep from *, end last repeat k4.

Row 39—With A, k3, * sl 1, k11, sl 1, k3; rep from *.

Row 41—With B, k2, * sl 1, k3, (sl 1, k1) 3 times, sl 1, k3, sl 1, k1; rep from *, end k1.

Row 43—With A, k5, * sl 1, k7; rep from *, end last repeat k5.

Row 44—See Row 2.

Repeat Rows 1–44.

Stepped Fret

Stepped Fret

Multiple of 10 sts plus 3. Colors A and B.

Cast on with Color A and knit one row.

Note: On all right-side (odd-numbered) rows, slip all sl-sts with yarn in *back*.

Row 1 (Right side)—With B, k1,* (sl l, k1) twice, sl, l, k5; rep from*, end sl 1, k1.

Row 2 and all other wrong-side rows—Knit (or purl) the same sts worked on previous row, with the same color; sl all the same sl-sts with yarn in *front*.

Row 3—With A, k6, * sl 1, k3, sl 1, k5; rep from *, end last repeat k2.

Row 5—With B, k1, * sl 1, k1, sl 1, k3, (sl 1, k1) twice; rep from *, end sl 1, k1.

Row 7—With A, k4, * (sl 1, k1) 3 times, sl 1, k3; rep from*, end last repeat k2.

Row 9—With B, k1, * sl 1, k5, sl 1, k3; rep from *, end sl 1, k1.

Row 11—With A, k2,* (sl 1, k1) twice, sl l, k5; rep from*, end k1.

Rows 13 and 14—With B, knit.

Rows 15 and 16—With A, repeat Rows 11 and 12.

Rows 17 and 18—With B, repeat Rows 9 and 10.

Rows 19 and 20—With A, repeat Rows 7 and 8.

Rows 21 and 22—With B, repeat Rows 5 and 6.

Rows 23 and 24—With A, repeat Rows 3 and 4.

Rows 25 and 26—With B, repeat Rows 1 and 2.

Rows 27 and 28—With A, knit.

Repeat Rows 1-28.

Index